Both Sides Now

By

Connie Corcoran Wilson

ISBN: 1-4107-8120-8 (e-book)
ISBN: 1-4107-8121-6 (Paperback)
ISBN: 1-4107-8122-4 (Dust Jacket)

This book is printed on acid free paper.

1stBooks - rev. 10/31/03

Table of Contents

INTRODUCTION

For forty-seven years, I have threatened to write "MY" book. This is it.

I began writing at age eleven, when I won fifty dollars for a poem submitted to an Archdiocese of Dubuque poetry contest by my sixth grade teacher at St. John's Elementary School in Independence, Iowa. Sister Mary Alphonsus had no idea what she had started! The poem was entitled "My Dream" and demonstrated that, even then, I at least understood the concept of writing for an intended audience. And, even then, I wrote poetry that, to this day, I refer to as "doggerel." But it's "MY" poetry, and it deserves its moment. So, here is Poem Number One:

"My Dream"

Last night was windy,
Last night was dark,
I had a dream,
That left its mark.

I saw a person whom I love,
Someone special who lives above.
I saw a vision of perfection,
One whose guidance gives protection.

OK. So, Shakespeare it's not. But I was only eleven at the time; give me a break! Fifty dollars was a lot of money for stringing a few words together in a poem, then or now! I was, as they say, "off and running." I was hooked.

When I reached junior high school, the editor of the Independence, Iowa, newspaper, the *Bulletin Journal &*

Conservative, a highly respected journalist by the name of Reeves Hall, asked my dad if I would write a regularly recurring series of feature stories for our small town newspaper. Dad started the local bank in 1941, with others recommended by the State Banking Board.

The concept was that a column written by a youngster would have appeal to readers, if only because it *was* written by a child. I was sent out to interview a farmer whose field represented the exact middle watershed point of the state; I interviewed Marie Turgasen's son, John, who had built his own telescope. Mrs. Turgasen was my high school English teacher and advisor of the school newspaper I was Editor-in-Chief of in my junior and senior years of high school.

I also worked on the newspaper and the yearbook alongside Janet (Harridan) Daily (later the world's fifth best-selling living author of numerous Harlequin romances). When I graduated, I was awarded a Ferner/Hearst Journalism Scholarship by the University of Iowa, based on a series of columns and articles written during my high school years, submitted by Mrs. Turgasen.

Mrs. Florence Helt, another of my high school English and speech instructors, helped shape my love of writing, as did the junior high teachers who had gone before her, including Miss Clara Scoggin, widely feared for her iron rule, and Mrs. Florence Peters. Mrs. Peters made us all write mock newspapers called "The Raveloe Times," based on the book *Silas Marner* by George Eliot. There may have been a more boring novel, but I don't remember what it was, unless it was Dickens' *Bleak House*, which I had the misfortune to have to read three times for three different college classes. (Never was so much written about so little).

Miss Scoggin was what we used to call an Old Maid. I think the official bank term when making loans was spinster. When I graduated, she sent me a hanky and a lovely graduation card. Very uncharacteristic of her. The only thing I remember about her eighth grade English class was that she chased Janet McHenry around the room, accidentally tripping and falling over a box of Christmas decorations. That, plus the day she asked Gary Ogdahl (now deceased) to use "inter" as a prefix in a sentence. Gary chose to use the word "intercourse." Very racy stuff, in those pre-MTV days! (Miss Scoggin was not amused.). It never occurred to me that Miss Scoggin thought I was a good student of English, but, looking back, I think she must have.

I became an English major at the University of Iowa and taught English to seventh and eighth grade students in Silvis, Illinois from 1969 until 1985. Along the way, I picked up a Master's and thirty additional hours in places as diverse as the University of California at Berkeley, Northern Illinois University, and Western Illinois University. In 1985, I accepted a position as an educational writer for Performance Learning Systems, Inc., of Emerson, N.J., a nationally known teacher training firm. In 1989, I co-authored their book *Training the Teacher As A Champion* and wrote their newsletter. Along the way, I have taught English and composition classes at every college or university in the Iowa/Illinois Quad Cities, six at last count. Currently, I am teaching "Communications Skills" and "Introduction to College Writing" at Eastern Iowa Community College's Scott County campus.

On November 15, 1986, I founded the Sylvan Learning Center in Bettendorf, Iowa. I sold it March 1 of 2002. I also lost my mother on May 2, 2002, and several friends and relatives died during this watershed year. When your contemporaries in their fifties are dropping like flies, the "some day" you had always planned for is now. My husband retired after thirty-six years with Deere & Company. It really is time for "MY" book. Forty-seven years is a long pregnancy.

So, friends and neighbors, I am assembling for your edification and amusement the humor columns I wrote in the mid-eighties, which were published in *The Rock Island Reminder* (Rock Island, Illinois) and *Metro East* (East Moline, Illinois) and in numerous other magazines. *Reader's Digest* almost ran the exercise piece I will lead off with, sending me a lovely letter regarding potential purchase and giving me the false promise of eventual fame and fortune. No such luck.

Some of these pieces stand up well to the test of time. Others seem "dated". But many represent what I was thinking twenty years ago, and my writing then was from an entirely different perspective than my writing now. So, the both sides of the title represent youth and maturity, as well as humor contrasted with darker emotions.

Since I have "looked at life from both sides now," as the song lyric goes, I have written a few current pieces to update and balance things out. These were written when I was a young teacher and housewife and are still being written now. They are both funny and serious. Since Bombeck-style humor is only one side of the literary coin, I have interspersed some original poems that are not intended to be "funny." I hope you enjoy. There will be more to come. I promise.

And it won't take forty-seven years.

Connie Corcoran Wilson, M.S.
March 31, 2003

My sincere thanks to Karen Burgess Schootman and Stephanie Wittmer, who proofread most of this book for me.

From left to right: Connie (Corcoran) Wilson; Mary Beth (Blakesley) Leytze; Barbara Overland; Cheryl Head; Bettie (Roehrkasse) Gerdes; Janet (Harridan) Daily. Cheerleaders in 1962-1963 at Independence High School.

ESP: EXERCISE STRESS POINTS

I have devised a point system similar to that scale used to tell when a person has too much stress in his or her life. My scale is designed to warn you when you have signed up for an exercise class that is too difficult for you.

On the life stress scale, a marriage, divorce, new baby or death in the family might equal 100 points. On my exercise stress point scale, you are assigned Exercise Stress Points (ESP) to signal when you are in a world of hurt.

For openers, you can always tell you're in serious trouble if you are the only one who looks like they really *need* the class and are the only one not wearing leg warmers. After that, the scale is as follows:

10 ESP (exercise stress points): Class assembles. Instructor leads vigorous calisthenics for a full twenty minutes. You are exhausted and turning blue. Just as you are about to collapse quietly in a corner, your group leader—-who always has a name like Bambi or Heidi—-chirps, "Now that we're all warmed up, let's begin our first set of exercises." This question flashes through your mind: when, exactly, did *her* exercises become *our* exercises?

20 ESP: You discover that the rest of the class has been working out at home to Jane Fonda's Advanced Exercise tape. You have been using a Debbie Reynolds record and "Sweatin' to the Oldies." Add five more ESP if you think Richard Simmons is "cute."

30 ESP: Your pants split up the back as you attempt to do a backwards roll.

40 ESP: Woman next to you on your left looks at your beet-red face and comments, "I see you're flirting with Old Mr. Blood Pressure."

50 ESP: When you are supposed to check your pulse to see if you have achieved your level of aerobic fitness, you cannot find yours. No one else can find your pulse, either. You hope this does not mean that you have been declared legally dead at some point during the last twenty minutes.

60 ESP: You begin to hyper-ventilate and are forced to put your head between your legs—-no easy task! Later, it takes two class members to remove your head from between your legs.

70 ESP: Food fantasies occupy your thoughts. Complete this sentence, "Gee, after all this, I can go up to Hagen Daaz and……." "Jog around the block" is not the phrase you would use to complete this sentence.

80 ESP: Woman on your right, having made contact with the funny bone in your right elbow with her exercise wand, says, "Excuse me. I'm a little out of practice. I just got out of the hospital yesterday; the quints are doing fine!"
    As the pain escalates, you try to decide whether to (A) steal her exercise wand after class and burn it as an offering to the Exercise God (if She exists), or (B) grab it out of her hand RIGHT NOW and break it over your knee. You opt for (B), grabbing and breaking.

90 ESP: You are ejected from the class and the club for willfully and wantonly destroying another class member's exercise wand. As you leave, with your pants gaping wide, you are heard muttering about the population explosion.

100 ESP: Your husband hits the roof. He discovers that your $500 health club membership fee is non-refundable once you have begun class AND you are billed $50 for the broken exercise wand!

(*Notes from the vantage point of twenty years later---- with credit for the expression to Bridget DeJonghe: I "can't want to" do yoga, either.)

LIFE

There are folks
Who never drink down life,
They sip it, like a tea.
Those people, with their pinkies out,
Those people, they aren't me!

I taste of life,
I drink it down,
I revel in its feel.
I shan't let "sensible" prevail
And life's best moments steal.

So, wear your rubbers,
Watch your back.
Beware the wild and crazy.
Do nothing to excite yourself.
Be fat and dumb and lazy.

Stake out the moral high ground,
Look down on those who don't,
Amuse yourself? Take looks around?
Please you?
It just won't.

The bravest of hearts,
The strongest of souls,
They face the night unafraid.
The timid of heart,
The weakest of souls,
Cannot even face the day.

9/14/96

FOR BAD LUCK, BIGGER IS BETTER

The carpet man came to replace my blue bathroom carpeting yesterday. The old carpeting was only two years old. It was barely worn and matched the wallpaper—-and had a burned spot the size of a dinner plate precisely in the middle!

All this came about when my handy dandy space heater shorted out just as I was about to step into the tub. Since I wasn't exactly dressed in my Smokey the Bear fire-fighting costume at bath-time and had no desire to ruin any good towels by putting a fire out with them, I quickly unplugged the heater, crouched on my hands and knees, and blew the flames out.

A charming sight, I assure you.

Two days before the carpetman was due to replace the burned blue carpeting, it rained in the night and flooded the basement bathroom, recently re-decorated in shades of orange.

So, while the carpet man was here repairing the burned blue carpeting, I asked him to take a look at the flooded orange carpeting. If it's not fire, it's flood.

"Geez, lady!" he hollered up from the basement," You've got a regular swamp down here! Have you contacted your insurance man?"

I dialed our insurance man, Alibi Ike. He informed me that the next time I set fire to the bathroom, "You should really torch it!" It seems that we have a $250 deductible on our insurance policy. The total repair bill was $236.74.

Ike, never a quick study, intoned, "Now…let me get this straight. You were struck by lightning?"

"Uh….no, Ike," I answered. "The lightning woke me up. It was rain or hail that did the damage. You can see the water marks on the window of the basement bathroom window well."

"Oh, gee. We don't cover water damage."

"Let me see if I have this right. You don't cover fire damage. You don't cover water damage. Just exactly what DOES this insurance cover, Ike, because I'd like to get some good out of it?"

"I hear you! I hear you! Did you say that there was hail damage?"

"I didn't, but I *can*, Ike. Would that help? Tell them it hailed on the carpet and dented it. Tell them anything you want, Ike, but get me some good out of this policy!" I hung up, feeling frustrated.

Just as I was feeling my most thwarted, news came of a woman who was driving oh-so-very-carefully across some bumpy railroad tracks in an attempt to keep the undercarriage of the family roadster in one piece.

Naturally, she had all the kids in the car, and, since she was being *very* careful not to hit any of the bumps too hard, she became stuck right in the middle of the tracks, just as a train approached.

She and I have to look on the bright side. I didn't burn the house down; she managed to get the kids out of the car right before the train totaled it.

Sometimes, bigger is better, like when you want to try to file an insurance claim.

Sometimes, you just have to make peace with your situation and move on.

RIDDLES

I cannot glean the answer
Of riddles from the past
Nor see the future clearly
By the shadow that it casts.
But I can feel the future coming,
Feel its breath upon my cheek,
Whispering of the sameness
That makes me sick and weak.

What, then, is the answer?
Or the question, truth to tell....?
Am I just to keep on walking
On this lonely path to hell?
I seek to forge a future
Holding hope and peace and light,
And passion for the living
Before the fall of night.

But the whispering just gets louder,
It echoes in my head.
I hope I find the answer,
Before I wake up dead.

12/31/95

To the Victims Go the Spoils

I found something that resembled grass in my refrigerator drawer this morning. It was either very moldy bacon or badly decomposed celery——take your pick. Even though it had an obnoxious odor and the consistency of slime, it wasn't nearly as odious as some of the things I save only to find them later——*much* later!

As one frequent dinner guest, a bachelor, said to me recently, "Oh, what the heck! I'll throw caution to the winds! Pass the salad dressing!"

I reminded him of two old sayings, "Beggars can't be choosers," and "The price is right."

He countered with his own saying: "To the victims go the spoils."

Citrus fruit seems to have a special affinity for going gray-green in my kitchen. Self-respecting oranges, like elephants, pick a spot to die: my hydrator drawer. Alexander Fleming, discoverer of penicillin, would think he had discovered the Mother Lode.

Grapefruit fare no better. Once a grapefruit, always a grapefruit. Unless it's a grapefruit in my refrigerator. I've tried passing them off as fuzzy shrunken basketballs for pygmies, but my family knows a decaying grapefruit when they smell one. They have a well-developed sixth sense about such things.

It is a well-known fact that Alexander Fleming accidentally discovered penicillin when he noticed a bit of mold had fallen from a culture plate in his laboratory and had destroyed bacteria around it. Less well-known is the fact that Fleming also discovered lysozyme, a substance found in human tears.

There is no truth to the rumor that Fleming discovered both while rutting around in my refrigerator on defrosting day.

Connie Corcoran Wilson

ANGER

I've so much anger deep inside,
That there's no room for love to hide.
"Kind" has died and gone to hell,
And "love" is going there, as well.

This helpless rage, this bitter ire,
Lights the spark, ignites the fire,
And from this useless bitter wrath
Comes a cold wind 'cross your path.

If you're among the target few
Here's what I suggest you do:
"Hold fast to love,
For if love dies…
Life's a bird that cannot fly."
A bird with feathers sad and gray,
Listless, drab by light of day.

I'd like to love
With all my heart,
But it's much too difficult to start.
So I'll just feel this anger grow,
It's all that I'm allowed to know.

9/4/96

KROEHLER'S SECRET

A young single girlfriend with the unusual first name of Pan stayed overnight with me in Iowa City at the time I was taking the State of Iowa Writers' Workshop two-week course. You should have heard me encouraging her visit.

"Come on up, Pan. Seriously! There'll be lots of single guys for you! The place'll be lousy with them! You'll love it! You can sleep on the hide-a-bed in my apartment. I'll take you out for dinner. I know a place where they have terrific food!"

When she arrived, tired from her long drive from the Twin Cities, she asked if she could take a short nap before dinner.

"Sure! No problem! It's nice and quiet around here."

The neighbors were felling a tree directly outside my bedroom window.

Dinner held no more luck for my visitor. The Chinese dish that Pan ordered from the menu at the restaurant was so bad the manager approached us, unbidden, asking, "How's your dinner?"

She reluctantly admitted that it tasted as though an entire bottle of soy sauce had been dumped in just one serving.

"We've had several complaints about it. It must be the new brand of soy sauce. We aren't serving it any more and would like to replace your meal."

After dinner, we discovered that Maxwell's and the Field House, two well-known Iowa City watering holes, were locked and dark. In our neighborhood on the way home, we couldn't even find a place to buy a cup of coffee——and it was only 10:30 p.m.

We tried Wendy's, a pizza place, and a bowling alley before we went to a grocery store and bought instant coffee to make back at my apartment.

When Pan and I tried to open the hide-a-bed, there was a little tag attached that said: "Kroehler——the couch with a secret."

The secret—-which is still safe with Kroehler—-was how to open the hide-a-bed!

There was one bright spot for a single girl during the evening, though. We did find a males-only convention in progress at our restaurant.

It was a convention of priests.

REFLECTIONS

I took my heart down off the shelf;
Examined it for cracks.
It seemed to have no major flaws.
And so I put it back.

It wasn't till much later, then,
I realized it was torn,
That insults to its inner core,
Had rendered it forlorn.

Where is the glue to heal such cracks,
To make it whole again?
Is there a formula somewhere
Residing with a friend?

What would you recommend to me
To fix my damaged soul?
Is there anything that one can buy
To really make it whole?

If you stumble on the answer
To this question I ask you,
Please let me know the remedy
So my spirit can be true.

NUMBER 401, VINCENT VAN GOGH, AND ME

Today, I had my ears pierced. It's something I've been building up the courage to do for more than a decade. I think of it as a symbolic act, a statement of my independence and maturity. My mother always disapproved of pierced ears in her own inimitable fashion and felt they were somehow "cheap" and vaguely gypsy-like.

I, on the other hand, had come to feel that all the truly smart, chic, uptown and stylish women had pierced ears. There was no room for compromise. I felt the way I did about going down Space Mountain at Disneyworld. I knew it was something I should do because it was supposed to be GREAT, but I also knew that I threw up after my last ride on the Tilt-a-Whirl. Hardly a recommendation for future rides. Never one to give in easily to peer pressure, I felt apprehensive and anxious. People who tried to allay my fears made me feel worse.

So, today, I went about deciding whether to pierce my ears very scientifically.

I flipped a coin.

Heads, I did it. Tails, I did not.

It came up heads. My teen-aged son Scott and I went back to the boutique advertising this special.

"Don't you want to go play video games?" I asked Scott, whose eyes are permanently glazed from such activity.

"No. I want to watch."

The young clerk—-Kathy by name—-seemed quite knowledgeable. No, the posts did not have to be 14K gold

14

these days. These were surgical steel and would work just as well. They were hypo-allergenic.

By this time, I was hyper-aller-nauseous.

After she had assured me that she had done over 400 people and had personally trained all her girls, I submitted, on condition that the store manager Kathy, herself, and one of her two young assistants, administer the coup de grace.

"Just what I need," I thought, "two more holes in my head."

Kathy carefully positioned me on the stool, explaining that, since I was obviously apprehensive (read: scared out of my mind) I should sit down so that I wouldn't fall down and hurt myself if I fainted.

That is somehow not a very reassuring statement at such moments.

This was followed by, "It would have been good for you to have brought another adult."

Hmmmmmm. Ominous.

I sat. She grabbed her trusty staple gun. I began verbally rattling aloud like a Chatty Cathy doll, figuring the date it would be when my six weeks of post-twirling and sterilizing would be up.

Six people had gathered to watch: two women, obviously as nervous as I, and three sober wide-eyed girls in their teens. And, of course, my first-born.

Kathy, in a voice like kindly old Doc Welby soothing a hysterical patient, said, "Now you're going to hear a loud click." I was glad that she hadn't said, "Now you are going to hear a LOUD boom."

I only heard a soft click above my nervous nattering and calculating.

Then I heard Kathy say, "Oh oh. This has never happened to me before. It didn't go all the way through."

Who knew I had the world's thickest ear lobes? I knew that 401 was not destined to be my lucky number.

I suggested to Kathy, who was, by now, sweating profusely, "You might as well go through with fixing it, Kathy. It's a little like childbirth. It's kind of hard to go back now! You know what I mean?" This brought a chuckle from the assembled crowd. Then, with a flash of inspiration fueled by fear, I said, "Of course, we could just hang a matching staple gun from my left ear and try to start a new fad."

The shop girls tried unsuccessfully to suppress their laughter.

I noticed that Kathy, who was sawing determinedly at the post and gun in my ear, did not laugh. She was muttering softly to herself. Something about being warned there'd be days like this, but why did they have to happen to her?

My ear was now the consistency and color of chopped liver, and I was trying that old dentist's chair stand-by: alternative pain to distract. There is no end to this story. Kathy put the left ear post in without incident, and I left, telling her that it was probably not her fault. Although, in these situations, whose fault is it, really? All three of the adult onlookers fled, although one of them ventured the opinion that I should have been given a free pair of earrings. Or ears. Whichever would be cheapest and easiest.

Kathy pretended not to hear that crack, just as she had pretended not to hear the suppressed laughter of her crack staff.

So, for a mere $10, I got a cauliflower ear and instant empathy with one of history's greats: Vincent Van Gogh.

Number 401, Vincent Van Gogh, and me.

Connie Corcoran Wilson

FOR JFK, JR.

Down to the sea, in ships, they go…
Words are uttered, low and slow,
Incantations fill the air,
"Dust to dust;" he was so fair.

His comely features grace our past,
His life a gift not meant to last,
His days are spent and gone, alas!
A life lived well, but gone too fast.

We know so little of our fate.
Will we be good? Will we be great?
Our lives are filled with love and hate.
There is no way to make Death wait.

"Why?" is the word that haunts us still.
"When?" is unanswered. We know not, till
He calls for us, on that dark night,
To take us on our final flight.

Live as though this were that day.
Live as though we had a say.
Make a difference: find a way!
Love all men so that you may.

(*This was written on my 54th birthday. Today, they buried the cremated remains of JFK, Jr., and his wife and sister-in-law, at sea, near where we will soon be on vacation in Westerly, Rhode Island. The brightest of the Kennedy lights, extinguished forever. No spark or ember to take his place. 7/23/99)

TEN RULES TO REMEMBER WHEN YOU ENTERTAIN

The following are Wilson's Ten Rules of Entertaining, or how to eat your heart out:

RULE 1: The number of guests shall always be one more than the number of matching plates.

RULE 2: The guests, when they equal the number of available matching cups or glasses, will misplace their cup and/or glass, requiring that a Jolly Olly Orange mug or a glass bearing a facsimile of either Porky Pig or Daffy Duck be pressed in to service.

RULE 3: If all the guests arrive, the pre-ordered hors d'oeuvres won't.

RULE 4: Gravy made for company will always either separate or have lumps.

RULE 5: The most important guest at a dinner party will always receive the chipped cup (every dinner service has one), no matter how carefully the hostess sets the table.

RULE 6: Chairs will mysteriously disappear just when they are needed most.

RULE 7: At least one guest will be allergic to whatever you serve; one will have a rare swallowing disorder that makes it necessary to have bland pablum, rather than the main entrée; and a whopping fifty per cent will be on strict diets.

RULE 8: Whatever is supposed to rise will fall, and whatever is supposed to fall will rise. This can be summarized as, "What goes up must come down——but please not until I've served the soufflé!"

RULE 9: Whatever the recipe calls for, you won't have it on hand. If you think you do have it on hand, you will discover at the last moment that the container is empty. The only convenience store open at this time of the evening will not have whatever it is.

RULE 10: If anything can be spoiled, dropped, burned, or lost, it will be if the event is an important dinner party. Conversely, perfect meals are the order of the day when only your own immediate family or people you hate are being served.

One restaurant actually *lost* a five-foot sandwich I had ordered for a party. How do you "lose" a five-foot sandwich?

There are several corollaries that accompany **Wilson's Rules of Entertaining**, which will be left for later. Among these are: never serve anything that was not green when you purchased it or moves when you open the box; don't throw oil on troubled waters or water on oil fires; and save the family photo album in the event of a kitchen three-alarmer. The closest we came to a three-alarm fire was the memorable pretzel-in-white-chocolate dipping party, which nearly resulted in third degree burns when Number One son caught the waxed paper on fire. He was oblivious. The flames were climbing up the waxed paper towards his arm while I stared, mesmerized. Somehow, I managed to grab his arm and the fork that had the waxed paper (which had adhered to the pretzel), still blazing, attached, and throw it (the fork, not the arm) in the sink. We later learned that his uncle, for whom we were making this delicacy as a Christmas present, hated white chocolate pretzels because he had once eaten an entire box by himself and became violently ill immediately thereafter. He thought it was some kind of cruel joke at his expense.

And you always thought the phrase, "Dinner will be ready when the smoke alarm goes off!" was a joke.

Connie Corcoran Wilson

YOUNG AND SILLY

Once, when I was young and silly,
A sweet, small thing….
A winsome filly…
Someone said to me, in jest,
"I care for you; I love you best."
That was all it took to do it:
Set me off and put me through it.

But now I'm older than before,
I've pretty much been through it,
I've heard the lies and gotten wise
And learned to say, "Oh, screw it!"
Am I glad I learned this way,
And became a major cynic?
It sure does beat the other way:
Committed to a clinic.

MY MOST MEMORABLE DINNER PARTY

I once invited four couples for a dinner that turned out to be doomed. It was, quite literally, the dinner party from hell!

It was near Thanksgiving, and I always make a twenty-pound bird for the entire family at Thanskgiving. From having done this every year since 1968, I have, imbedded in my admittedly lame memory bank, the information that turkeys take "twenty minutes to the pound.." Who needs to look up stuff you already "know?" However, I was planning to use our new microwave to fix a turkey breast, and, of course, in the microwave, it takes much, much less time. I found this out the hard way.

I put the turkey breast in the microwave and set it for the appropriate amount of time *for the conventional oven*. Who knows how long that was? One hour? Two hours? Then, I went back to my hostessing chores, which consisted largely of drinking wine in a separate room off the kitchen and conversing with my guests.

When the smoke alarm went off, I discovered that there was a football-shaped object in my microwave that was about the size of a football. It was completely black and charred. It was smoking.

I tried, delicately, to get my husband to join me in the kitchen, so that we could discuss this problem. He, of course, was oblivious, having *really* gotten in to helping me with my hostessing chores, i.e., drinking.

Finally, he came to the kitchen only to agree with me that the turkey was a goner.

I sent him out for Colonel Sanders' chicken, which, conveniently, went with everything else we were having (stuffing, scalloped corn, mashed potatoes, etc.)

As we gathered to pass the bucket and chow down, a mouse ran through my dining area, immediately under the large round oak table at which we were seated. Every woman in the place screamed, and, like the June Taylor Dancers on crack, jumped, in unison, on to their chair seats.

People still mention this dinner party to me. I don't know why.

I tell them that my father, years earlier, had predicted a bright future for me in the kitchen. I left a light-weight aluminum pan on an electric stove burner and left to go swimming. As I recall, this large pot had some water in it at some point. Obviously, I did not realize that I had left the burner on to depart for several hours of swimming.

When I returned home, all the windows in our kitchen were out....I mean OUT. Literally.The glass was gone and smoke was pouring from the windows. Firemen were present. The water in the pan had boiled dry and then the aluminum pan apparently melted and, drop by aluminum drop, dripped into the innards of our electric stove.

My father took the cooled fifty-cent sized piece of aluminum and drilled a hole in it and gave it to me, saying, "Whoever gets you for a wife is going to really have their work cut out for them, since you can't even boil water." He said this with a smile, I think, glad that I had not set the entire house on fire.

I am a pretty good cook today, but I can't promise anything, as far as long-term damage to the kitchen. To prove my versatility as a cook, however, I shall include my lasagna recipe for your perusal. It is, without a doubt, the best lasagna you will ever make, if you are one-half Irish, one-fourth Norweigan and one-fourth Dutch:

The Great Wilsoni's World Famous Lasagna Recipe

Ingredients for the meat sauce:

2 lbs. ground chuck
3   six-oz. cans of tomato paste
1   sixteen-oz can of tomatoes
2   tablespoons minced parsley
3   tablespoons basil or oregano (use the leafy kind, if possible)
1 and ½ teaspoons garlic salt (to taste)
Be browning this stuff and tasting it frequently and throwing things in, as advised below. This means that you will always keep them guessing about what, exactly, is in it. If you are totally Germanic and anal and have to know EXACTLY what is in it, then you can stick EXACTLY to the recipe, but, I'm telling you, it won't be as good. So there.

Ingredients for the white sauce:

Cottage cheese – 4 cups of the large curd kind; (you can use that low-fat stuff if you are a glutton for punishment, but what is really the point?)
2 or 3 beaten eggs…use your own judgment. (Sometimes, I use 2; sometimes, I use 3. I don't like

to be pinned down. It depends on how large the egg is, perhaps.)

¾ teaspoons of salt

2 Tb. of parsley

½ cup of Parmesan cheese

½ tsp of seasoned pepper (use the kind that is made up of all those various different-colored peppers; it looks more appetizing. And, while cooking the meat sauce, frequently sprinkle some more dried parsley flakes).

Mix the above up in a medium-sized bowl and set it aside until the assembly phase.

1 lb. of Mozzarella cheese; I buy the grated kind. You will be using ½ in the middle and ½ on top.

While the meat sauce is cooking, taste it frequently and throw in things like seasoned salt, garlic salt, oregano, basil, rosemary, dried parsley…really, anything that suits your fancy, in small amounts. Also, be *very* careful about not OVER-salting. That is really about the only thing that can ruin this dish, unless you drop the entire pan upside-down, like my daughter's friend, Amanda, once did on the way into my son's apartment in Chicago.

Boil a box of lasagna noodles while making the two sauces above.

Assembly:

I am sure all of you have assembled lasagna before, but, just to be sure, let's review, class:

First, figure about 4 and ½ to 5 lasagna noodles per layer, with a bottom layer and a middle layer of noodles. Don't end with noodles on the top. End with meat sauce on top and mozzarella cheese over that. The noodles-on-top thing looks tacky.

We once had a lasagna cook-off at my house. Somebody brought a lasagna with the noodles ON TOP. Gack! Looked awful. Nobody wanted to eat it. As I recall, during the lasagna cook-off we had judges and everything and we put a bachelor friend up to "entering" a pan of lasagna that we purchased from Valentino's and passed off as his own. Valentino's no longer exists in my neck-of-the-woods and my lasagna beat it, anyway. Valentino's came in second.

Start with a layer of noodles. [In my pan, it takes about 4 to 5 noodles, per layer.]

Then, follow with a layer of white sauce.

Then, follow with a layer of meat sauce (1/2)

Then, use ½ of the Mozzarella cheese.

Now, put a SECOND layer of noodles in the middle, making sure that the noodles sort of "overlap" each other and that they don't go up the sides of the pan where they might burn and crust up. You want them covered with ingredients. Tuck them under the wet stuff if they stick out at any time.

When you finish off the assembly, you should put the white sauce first and the meat sauce last. Why? BECAUSE

I SAID SO AND THIS IS MY RECIPE! That white sauce or the noodles on top looks really unappetizing.You need to end with that red-meat sauce and mozzarella melting over that. After you have spread the last of the meat sauce on top of this concoction, sprinkle it with parsley flakes and that seasoned pepper, add the mozzarella cheese and freeze it, if you aren't going to have it immediately. It will weigh about 1 ton. I'm not kidding you. It will be very, very heavy.

Cook it for at least one hour in a 375 degree oven. My oven is very slow. It always takes an hour, minimum…sometimes more.

Let the lasagna sit briefly before cutting it.

Bon appetit!

A SOLE IN DISTRESS

I have a lot of trouble with shoes. You might say that, over the years, more than once I have been "a sole in distress."

My mother constantly chided me, in my youth, to buy "sensible shoes." What are "sensible shoes?" Shoes are inanimate objects; I never expected them to make sense. I never spent long hours locked in dialogue with my sneakers. There have been times, though, that I have directed some harsh remarks to an offending pair.

For example, there was the time in the sixties, in college, when I got the three-inch spike heel of my black suede pumps caught in a street grating while walking to church. For a short period, I imagined myself entering church barefoot or wearing a 4-foot square grill attached to my left heel. There was the time that my toddler son got his foot firmly wedged in the supermarket cart undercarriage. Never one to do things the easy way, I laid the cart on its side in the supermarket aisle to dislodge it. Later, it occurred to me that I could have simply had him slip his foot from the shoe, but, by then, I had chosen the less efficient method and a crowd had gathered. Once, while at a discotheque dancing, the strap on a pair of black patent leather flats broke. I learned that it is impossible to safety pin the strap and continue dancing with this repair technique.

Perhaps the most unusual episode, until now, was the New Year's Eve that television star Vicki Lawrence's mother tried to buy the fancy dress shoes I was wearing right off my feet at Lawry's, the famous Los Angeles eatery. It was weird and had something to do with them being a 7AAA, which isn't even my size. I had kicked them off while waiting for hours, and, when I went to retrieve them, Mrs. Lawrence was on the banquette in front of the glitzy shoes and noticed the odd size, which was, apparently, hers, even if it wasn't mine. I don't know why I bought 7AAA shoes when my true size was 5 and ½ "B" width. They were there. I liked them. It defies logic, as all my shoes purchases do. They were the Everest of shoes.

While in Hawaii over Easter break we went to see Bill Cosby perform at the Maui Hyatt. In order to get to the concert, we had to park about a mile away on a golf course and walk in through a back door. While we were crossing the golf course, the automatic sprinkler system kicked in, thoroughly soaking the grass and us. Coincidentally, this final day of our trip, confident that we had somehow avoided the sun god's wrath for the prior eight days, all three of us had received serious sunburns. The tops of my feet were beet red, and nylons were out of the question. In fact, the only shoes that I could tolerate, at all, on my red, swollen ankles, were a pair of soft cloth slings which were, figuratively and literally, on their last legs.

After we hit the golf course sprinkler system...or it hit us....one shoe kissed its sole goodbye. The top of the shoe was attached at the heel only, flopping around like Clarabelle the Clown's over-sized shoes. Ever ingenious, I tried chewing an entire pack of Juicy Fruit in thirty seconds and doing one of those Heloise repair jobs, which never work when you most need them. (Where is Martha Stewart when you really need her? Probably at her broker's.)

"COME ON!" my impatient and unsympathetic spouse yelled at me, as I stood there, chipmunk cheeks crammed with gum, chewing furiously. "We've only got five minutes! You'll just have to carry them."

That is how I happened to attend a show at one of the world's most elegant hotels barefoot. I swept past the tuxedo-clad usher at the $80 million resort with the $35 million art collection, concealing my shoes beneath my wrap. The usher barely glanced at my very respectable long dress, but he did a double-take on the bare toes peeking out from under the hem, shook his head, and mumbled, under his breath, "Tourists!"

Summoning up whatever shred of dignity I could muster, I pulled myself up to my full five-foot three-inch height (OK....5' 2 and ¾") and followed the insolent usher to my seat in a ballroom crowded with bejeweled women in high heels.

Table ninety-one is a loooooong walk when you're dodging the spiked heels of others while trying to appear nonchalant and carrying, rather than wearing, your shoes. But a sole in distress just needs confidence to pull it off.

Connie Corcoran Wilson

Burned Steel

Life is such a constant sorrow,
Living with it, day by day,
Realizing that, on the morrow,
Things will still be just this way.

It is hard for us to realize....
It doesn't feel like it is "real,"
But, to the families of the victims,
It must feel burned, just like the steel.

Steel is thought to be impervious
Strong and resolute it is
So, we went on, all oblivious,
Never saw the lurking threat.

Steel is mighty; steel is strong;
Steel will hold great buildings up.
We did not know the aerodynamics
Of horror, hiding in our midst.

We didn't know that evil lived here
In the hearts of average men
We thought that all who lived here
Embraced peace and good will towards men.

Now we know that all aren't like us,
In this world, there are such things,
Now we know that steel cannot
Protect us from the lunatic fringe.

9/11/01 (After the World Trade Center bombing).

Major League Bugs

They sprayed for bugs in my junior high school classroom during Easter vacation. I know, because all the students were told to remove their books from their lockers prior to the spraying. I also know because the brown spray residue is still all over my classroom floor. It's right across the room from the spot where the roof leaks and forms a small lake when it rains.

When I say "bugs," I don't mean measly gnats. Oh, no! I'm talkin' major league cockroaches the size of a Buick, here, which we have euphemistically dubbed "water bugs." That is because they have been observed doing the backstroke in the lake.

I have a theory about these bugs. I think they are responsible for the books that keep disappearing. The cockroaches are carrying them off and stockpiling them. That may even be why the kids were told to remove their books from their lockers. No fools, these administrators, they wanted to keep the books out of the hands.....er, feelers....of the cockroaches.

Why would cockroaches want books? To keep them away from the termites that are eating the library bookshelves, of course. Yes, the crafty cockroaches know that if the termites corner the book food supply, the cockroaches have had it. And we're talking more than just food for thought here, folks!

So, the cockroaches have joined forces with the ants to stockpile their own source of book food. Ants, you say? Yes, ants. In the spring, I always have at least one fully developed anthill in my classroom. Two years ago it was directly behind my desk where I could point the little fellows out to my classes as object lessons in industry. Unfortunately, last year, the ants foolishly located near the lake in the back of the room. I think they were seeking to improve the property value of their hill. Break dancing students on their lunch hour killed the social-climbing ants that weren't flooded out.

The ants and the cockroaches have a Master Plan to outwit the library termites. Besides the locker books, which they have already infested and carried off, they are taking over the teachers' lounge. Ants in the sugar jar and pop bottles are a commonplace sight, but the cockroaches have really begun a full-scale assault. Last week, they captured Mr. Coffee Hill and a large, very dead cockroach was found, feet up, right in the middle of the community popcorn bowl.

What really brought all this home to me was when I absent-mindedly dropped a hunk of butter in the Pyrex measuring cup and popped it in to the microwave. Removing the cup, I discovered a sautéed cockroach, still sizzling in its own juices. Eeeeeuuuuwwwww!

Employees in the upper echelons of the work world just don't know what they're missing in fringe benefits because they didn't go in to education!

My most horrible suspicion concerning the cockroaches, ants and missing textbooks is a truly frightening prospect. What if they're founding an alternative school? They may even be using their own version of the ABC's—-Ants, Beatles and Cockroaches. They could be preaching insurrection right now and enlisting the aid of bookworms.

Spread the word.

Day of Infamy

The plumes of fire and smoke engulfed the sky,
Before our eyes the spires toppled to the ground.
Symbol of hate unleashed upon us——why?
The lives shattered midst this ungodly sound.

The world requires answers for those who fell
So that our souls aren't left to cope in fear
Of pain and grief and rage which mimic hell
And leave us lost to those ideals held dear.

The strong, the free, the brave, the best are we
Our nation's future rests upon this rock.
This land is built on hope, on liberty,
And this vile act cannot turn back the clock.

Our hearts are sad but firm in unity
We shall not rest, but mourn this memory.
1/11/01

C.W.

(*Shakespearian sonnet)

Plastic versus Paper

Friends, grocers, countrymen, lend me your ears! I come to bury plastic bags, not to praise them.

How many of you have noticed the creeping epidemic of plastic bags instead of paper bags at your friendly neighborhood supermarket checkout counter? I hate these sleazy-looking slimy plastic bags. A plastic bag won't stand upright all by itself, like a good old brown paper bag will. A plastic bag, by its very nature, contributes to the trash problem by becoming trash immediately after you empty it.

Oh, sure, if you want to invest additional money in some sort of special hardware to make a bag re-usable, you can, but, by itself, in its virgin state, a plastic bag is a bust.

A paper bag, by contrast, has many uses. It can be used to line a garbage can and helps eliminate trash, not add to it. They can be used to wrap packages for mailing. They are a key ingredient in my Salvation Army sorting sprees as they stand bravely at attention, awaiting cast-off but still serviceable items. A plastic bag would be lying down on the job. Paper bags are useful for various crafts, including making kits and paper airplanes. Some famous writers like Emily Dickinson used to scribble their poems on paper bags and old envelopes. None other than Abe Lincoln himself is supposed to have written his Gettysburg Address on the back of an old envelope…(but enough of envelopes, back to bags).

Plastic bags have puny little handles, which you are supposed to use to hoist the sack and its contents. The way my grocery bags always are filled to overflowing, there's no way this could work.

You can make a mask out of a paper bag. Or, if your date is exceedingly ugly, you can put a bag over her or his head. As Rodney Dangerfield used to say, he often had blind dates who were two-baggers. A two-bagger, said Dangerfield, was when your date was so ugly that you put a bag over her head and then put a bag over your own head, so that nobody would know that you were going out with this person. Try Dangerfield's two-bagger technique with these new-fangled plastic bags and you'd really be in danger. You'd wind up one-half of a murder/suicide.

If God had meant grocers to use these plastic grocery store travesties, there would be some sort of sign. Having the handles rip off your plastic bag, as mine did recently, and watching one dozen eggs smash on the sidewalk is not my idea of a favorable omen for the future success of these sleazy plastic grocery bags.

I have a good idea. Let's keep using the faithful old trusty brown paper bag. After all, as a much wiser person than I once ungrammatically said, "If it ain't broke, don't fix it!"

Mrs. Malaprop Lives!

Some two hundred years ago an English author named Richard Brinsley Sheridan wrote a play entitled "The Rivals," in which a comic character called Mrs. Malaprop appeared.

Mrs. Malaprop tried to impress people by using big words. Unfortunately, she usually chose an incorrect word or expression that only sounded like the correct one.

Audiences laughed when Mrs. Malaprop ordered her niece to pursue a man "at the very pineapple of success" or told her to "illiterate" another man from her memory.

Modern-day malapropism is alive and well. Norm Crosby, the stand-up comic, has made a good living from this type of humor for years. I have painstakingly saved a few from my many years of junior high school teaching.

From a student paper: "Michael Jackson will be around for a very long time. I think he might even beat Elvis in population." (The student was right about Michael Jackson being around for a very long time; his original nose, however, is not.)

"I stayed overnight with Bobby and we would go outside after his parents went to sleep and make a big bomb fire." (Must have been some fire!)

"I think if a nuclear war comes around, there will be survivors, but maybe after a month or two there will be kayos." (Yes. And there could be technical knock-outs, too!)

"When I am caught misbehaving, I get a good threshing." (I hope they use John Deere farm implements for this, although it sounds very painful.)

"My mom told me to turn my stereo down a few hundred disciples." (I often tell my daughter to turn her stereo down a few disciples, but it rarely does any good.)

"I told my little brother to quit playing records on my pornograph." (Ah, yes. The old pornograph.)

"The lady was in such poor condition that she needed artificial perspiration in the ambulance." (Right Guard, anyone?)

"Our coach yelled at us and said, 'You guys played like you were in a transom out there today!'" (Let's let that mental image sink in!)

"A good farmer must know how to irritate his crops." (It doesn't hurt if he knows how to irrigate them, either. I HATE when your crops get all testy after being irritated.)

From a Silvis School Board meeting of yesteryear and the lips of board member Bob Copeland: "I was in the hospital with a health problem so I've been pretty much incognito." Later, Bob said that he had "gone in to conclusion." (He pretty much has, now, since he's dead.) I think it was the very same board meeting where Mr. Ross pronounced "parochial" as "paro-chee-al" while reading from an issue of "Ladies' Home Journal," that Bible of education. Oh, those wacky board members of the seventies! Oh, the hilarity!

"We've got to find out who's making these unanimous phone calls!"

(Yes. And it wouldn't hurt to find out who's making the anonymous ones, as well.)

"Stop trying to invade the issue!" (When they get to Poland, we'll unite to stop them.)

"I just told you one of the great antidotes of all time, and you act like you're in a comma." (Oh, those pesky commas….the bane of all English students!)

Just last week, ABC's World News tonight used closed captioning to report that Alan Greenspan, the Federal Reserve Chairman, was recovering from surgery "to remove an enlarged prostitute." As reported in the May 5th, 2003, issue of *Time* magazine, his wife, NBC correspondent Andrea Mitchell, responding to the blooper, said, "He should be so lucky!"

And, not to be out-done by faux pas on the national level, the local newspaper had a similar moment. In the April 30, 2003 issue of Davenport, Iowa's *Quad City Times* a report ran on a suicide bomber's attack in Tel Aviv, Israel. Three people were killed and forty-six injured in the attack at Mike's Place on the seafront walkway in Tel Aviv, according to the article. As the history of such attacks was relayed, the article concluded by saying, "On June 1, 2001, a suicide bomber blew himself off in front of a disco at the southern end of the walkway, killing twenty-one people, most of them teenagers." A very sad story, but a humorous misprint, nonetheless.

In my junior high school teaching days, as a side job, I used to be sent out to interview local radio and television personalities, asking them about their on-the-air bloopers. There were stories from reporters who reported the fall of the Berlin wall as "a wall of drips, bricking with mortar." There was one poor slob who referred to "Korean Var weterans."

And speaking of veterans (or weterans), veteran Channel Four (WHBF) sportscaster Don Sharp was doing play-by-play at one basketball game when, noticing that the player was consistently undershooting the basket, he announced, "His shorts are all shot." Quickly realizing his error, he recovered by adding, "Come to think of it, his shoes don't look so hot, either." Sharp also had the distinction of mispronouncing the word "putting" in saying, (while covering a golf tournament), "Here we have Mrs. _____ putting out on the 18th hole." Just one small change in one vowel, and look what happens!

At basketball sectional tournament time in the state of Iowa, Tia Slater (then of KWQC, Channel 6, the NBC affiliate) says that a colleague turned to her at the news desk during the 10 o'clock news and said, "Well, Tia, it looks as though we have a lot of girls' sexual activity here in the state of Iowa tonight."

Fellow KWQC newsman Alan Byrn told a funny story that went like this: "I was announcing the change in a stadium playing surface from astro-turf to real grass and I said, 'The change from artificial grass to natural gas is right on schedule.'"

Bill Baker, who used to grace the air-waves as Bryan McGannon on what was then WQUA radio (1230 AM) once started his ad for a clothing store this way. "I snapped on the mike with real authority," remembers Baker, "and announced: 'Attention! Fart small shoppers!'"

Shades of Mrs. Malaprop.

If You Cannot Find Osama: Bomb Iraq!

Just before we did the "shock and awe" number, dropping tons and tons of smart bombs on Iraq on April 9, 2003, I was sent this e-mail message by a friend of a friend. I found the ditty to be right on in its message, which was as follows:

(Sung to the tune of "If You're Happy and You Know It")

If you cannot find Osama, bomb Iraq.
If the markets are a drama, bomb Iraq.
If the terrorists are frisky,
Pakistan is looking shifty,
North Korea's much too risky:
Bomb Iraq!

Although we have no allies with us: Bomb Iraq!
If we think someone has "dissed" us, Bomb Iraq!
So, to hell with the inspections,
Let's look tough for the elections,
Close your mind and take directions: Bomb Iraq!

It's "pre-emptive non-aggression": Bomb Iraq!
To prevent "mass destruction": Bomb Iraq!
They've got weapons we can't see
And that's good enough for me
'Cause it's all the proof I need: Bomb Iraq!

If you never were elected: Bomb Iraq!
If your mood is quite dejected: Bomb Iraq!

If you think Saddam's gone mad,
With the weapons that he had,
AND HE TRIED TO KILL YOUR DAD!
Bomb Iraq!

If your corporate fraud is growin': Bomb Iraq!
If your ties to it are showing: Bomb Iraq!
If your politics are sleazy,
And hiding it ain't easy,
And your manhood's getting queasy: Bomb Iraq!

Fall in line and follow orders: Bomb Iraq!
For our might knows not our borders: Bomb Iraq!
Disagree? We'll call it treason,
Let's make war, not love, this season,
Even if we have no reason: Bomb Iraq!

This contribution amused me mightily, and I took it with me to my volunteer reading to the visually disabled on WVIK, sharing it with the young clerk who was the night watchman of the shift. I had been reading to the blind and visually impaired, as a good deed, for over a year. It had come to my attention that even the blind and visually impaired might be bored to near-death or coma by one entire hour filled with nothing but grocery prices and/or obituaries. So, during the three-minute break we were entitled to take at the half hour, I would normally bring in something "funny" from the newspaper. The Dave Barry article on "The Twelve Days of Christmas", for example, and why it is a horrible song…a sentiment with which I am in complete agreement.

Nobody had ever noticed or commented upon the fact that, during MY three minutes, I would (occasionally) digress and read something other than an obituary (The obituaries are "the favorite show." I'm wondering if the listeners are just making sure that they're not in them.)

The Big Rule in radio, of course, is "no dead air" and the other rule is that you not vary from the format. But the three minutes of air-time at the half hour were mine, all mine, and I determined that my not-yet-dead listeners, all three of them, who were, no doubt, huddled together in front of their special receivers in a tiny closet in Silvis or Colona or Milan somewhere, might enjoy hearing this little ditty. It was not a subversive act. I didn't even attempt to make it a secret act, telling John (the student watchman) of this humorous piece and singing a verse for him, before I entered the booth.

The night all hell broke loose was the first night that WVIK (Augustana College's public radio station) had installed its new equipment. Normally, nobody listens to anyone on the air at any time, I am convinced, but, because they were having trouble regulating the volume levels of the new equipment, an engineer was (apparently) listening that night. I was only the second person to use the "new" equipment, which had been eagerly awaited for months, if not years.

Just as I launched in to the second stanza of "If You Cannot Find Osama, Bomb Iraq" an engineer, who, henceforth, shall be dubbed "a pin-headed engineer" (actually, it was his shirt that was pin-striped, but who's keeping score, really?) burst in to my cubicle, frantically making the universally known "cut" gesture at the neckline and practically foaming at the mouth. Geez!

I carefully turned the button to place the channel on the "network," which meant that pre-canned music would further anaesthetize the blind and almost-dead who were listening, picked up my things, and left. After all, I was an unpaid volunteer and the unpleasantness of this guy's frenzy cannot be over-stated.

Mr. Pinhead then flew after me, following me in to the parking lot, frothing with indignation, and quoting "FCC" this, that and the other thing. It was snowing outside at the time. I said, "Calm down or you'll have a stroke." Then, I got in my car and drove away. When he followed me the second time, I think I said, "Chill and get a life," but I really don't remember. It was cold. He was sputtering something about agreeing with me "in principle" but upholding until death the FCC, and I was freezing.

At the bottom of the hill, I realized that I had left my sweater in the broadcast booth. I drove back up the hill to retrieve it. There were now *five* "engineers" all huddled together outside the door of the studio. They were all a-flutter-twit! As I entered I said, "Gee! This must be the most excitement you guys have had in years!" My favorite engineer, Gary, quickly ducked his head and scurried down the hall, but Mr. Pinhead, again, pursued me in to the parking lot, practically apoplectic. It was all "FCC this" and "FCC that." Interestingly enough, although I made several subsequent phone calls to various mucky mucks, trying to find out exactly WHAT the FCC "rules and regulations" might have been, they could never be located. I probably would have to correspond with Colin Powell's son personally (the head of the FCC) to find out what horrible fate awaited someone like me, who dared to sing a satirical ditty on the air that was not politically correct at this moment in our nation's history, when we are all about marching in to countries that were leaving us alone and taking them over.

About this time, various anti-war demonstrations were taking place. I chose to join the one at the Writers' Studio, which I knew would be full of people who might be very full of themselves, many of them pontificating on the subject of war in "original" verse. The original verse was pretty bad, in general. Only Lawrence Ferlinghetti's poem held my attention. When I got out my accordion and invited the crowd to join me in a sing-along let's just say that it got their attention!

I had inherited the accordion from my cousin Lois's husband Larry on the Fourth of July, when we traveled to St. Louis to visit him for the last time, as he was terminally ill with liver cancer. Larry and I had for years shared a secret hatred of the accordion, which both of us were forced to learn to play against our will. We smuggled his old accordion down from the attic and in to the trunk of our car while my husband was in the bathroom. Since then, I had been having a great deal of fun getting it out and thinking up devilish ways to use it. This was one.

I also remember that each and every other participant in that night's event spent at least ten minutes introducing themselves, going on about how they taught here or taught there. (One guy said he had written six plays, to which I said, to the person seated next to me, "I don't think that Neil Simon has anything to worry about.") As I write this, there is no college or university, locally, that I have not been affiliated with, in one capacity or another. I, however, chose to remain anonymous. And so it was that, in the next morning's paper, as it wrote up the event, it said, "An anonymous woman with an accordion took the podium." And the paper went on to recite the first couple of stanzas of "If You Cannot Find Osama: Bomb Iraq!"

When I came home late from "tacos", my husband wanted to know where I had been. I said, "I was playing my accordion at an anti-war rally." He said, "Sure you were," rather wryly.

I also made a stand-up appearance at our local comedy club on the final Wednesday of February. I worked this in during the Wednesday night "taco night" with the girls, so that my husband was none the wiser. Our marriage is politically a little like that of Arnold Schwarzenegger and Maria Shriver, so I try to keep a low profile, whenever possible.

I included a lot of political humor in my Penguin's Club routine, along the lines of, "What did Gennifer Flowers say, when asked if her affair with Bill Clinton was similar to that of Bill and Monica Lewinsky?"

A: "Close, but no cigar."

I also shared the joke that historians had decided to call Clinton's eight years in office "Sex Between the Bushes." But never mind about that.

On that last Wednesday in February at Penguin's Comedy Club, it was my singing of "If You Cannot Find Osama, Bomb Iraq!" that was the featured set-piece of the evening's festivities. My tale of how Mr. Pin-headed (ok, pin-striped) Engineer Person pursued me into the parking lot of WVIK (next time: mace, I said) was greeted with chuckles. I also told about the after-math of my "faux pas" on the air.

The morning after I "dared to be different" on the air, I got a phone call from the woman who was the volunteer coordinator. Unfortunately, the woman chose to call me at 8:00 a.m. and it is well-known that calls to me before 10:00 a.m. are ill-advised. She went in to a long, droning speech about how we couldn't have this sort of shenanigans on the air. I was half asleep and so tired that, at one point, I laid the telephone down on the pillow next to me until the droning stopped. Then, I picked up the phone and shared the information with the nice lady that if Mr. Pin-headed Engineer Person pursued me in to the parking lot while yapping at my heels one more time, I would be forced to use mace. Or, barring that, that I would kick him right in the balls. I cheerily asked her to pass this information along to Mr. Pin-headed Engineer Person.

I also spent futile hours making phone calls to various mucky mucks affiliated with the station, in an attempt to find out exactly what the FCC "rules and regulations" actually were. I remember asking, "Was it my singing? Was that what set him off?"

I never found out what the FCC rules and regulations were. After the early-morning phone call from the previously nice (now decidedly frosty) volunteer lady, I got a letter from her, warning me that political commentary of this sort had no place in a democracy, since my opinion did not support our fearless leader's (George W.'s) bombing of a nearly defenseless country that hadn't attacked us.

After we actually bombed these poor schmucks back to the Stone Age, in keeping with George W. Bush's "Whack-A-Mole" foreign policy commitment (that is what the experts actually call it), I gave up any thought that the lives of innocent civilians and servicemen could be saved by the likes of me, and quit singing "If You Cannot Find Osama, Bomb Iraq!" But I still think it's a keen song, and I want to give public credit to the author of the poem, whoever he is, and say, "Hey! The blind and visually-impaired listeners with a special receiver within a 10 mile radius of WVIK in Rock Island, Illinois, are behind you!"

I also wrote a letter to the previously nice volunteer coordinator lady, saying that I didn't really think that the walls of WVIK would come tumbling down because I sang two stanzas of "the forbidden song," as I now call this ditty, which goes right there in the annals with the "forbidden dance," the Lambada.

And, if all else fails, and you *cannot* find Osama: Bomb Iraq! Nothing of value left there now, anyway.

The author, wearing Heidi braids, practicing for her anti-war rally accordion solo, another chance to trot out "If You Cannot Find Osama: Bomb Iraq!".

HOOTERS I & HOOTERS II

Hooters I:

I am not sure when Hooters became a factor in my life.

Was it when one of my son's girlfriends, in an unsuccessful bid to make him jealous and stampede him towards matrimony, took a second job there? She was commuting to Hooterville from her day job with an insurance agency and getting only four hours of sleep. The Hooters job did not last long. Still, it caused several humorous comments. My son was not that amused, and the relationship soon faltered. But Hooters had jiggled its way into my consciousness, even though I had never been inside a Hooters restaurant.

I saw the inside of a Hooters restaurant for the first time on September 11, 2001. I was at a Sylvan Learning Center conference in Baltimore, Maryland, in what is known as the Inner Harbor, residing on the thirty-eighth floor of Baltimore's tallest hotel, directly across the street from Baltimore's version of New York City's World Trade Center. Terrorists had just hit the twin towers of New York City with commercial airliners. I was mesmerized by the sight, "live," on my morning television screen. I realized that life as we knew it would never be the same again.

I had just come out of the bathroom clad in only a towel. I sank to the bed, still wearing only a towel. I didn't leave my room for hours, watching both assaults on the Twin Towers "live" until I was called by my employee, Chris, from the hotel lobby.

"Aren't you coming down?" she asked. It was now about noon and all the carnage had taken place early in the morning of that fateful day.

I explained that there wasn't a workshop or a Sylvan speaker of any kind who could hold my attention when history was being made on television and our world was seemingly spinning out of control. First, there were the two planes hitting the Trade Center. Then, there were reports of a plane hitting the Pentagon and another going down in Pennsylvania. No one knew what to expect or how big this conspiracy might be.

Chris, my faithful employee, repeated, "Aren't you coming down?"

I explained that I was still glued to my TV set, and I wondered aloud how it was that anyone would leave their set at this critical moment in our nation's history.

She said, "Well, maybe that's because they evacuated every floor above the fourth floor hours ago. The authorities aren't sure whether there are any other Eastern seaport cities that have been targeted by the terrorists, and they are taking the precaution because this is the tallest building in Baltimore, directly across the street from *their* World Trade Center."

Oh. Well. Nobody had 'splained it to me like THAT before!

So, I quickly gathered up what worldly belongings I thought I might need if I were barred from returning to my room for a long period of time, realizing, as I stuffed a book and writing material and comfortable walking shoes in to my tote bag, that I was hungry. I thought of the Alzheimer's documentary, where the elderly afflicted woman had packed only a telephone and bananas. My packing was beginning to resemble that degree of forethought. I was still reeling in shock.

This is where Hooters comes in, again. The city of Baltimore had come to an almost complete halt, like a flower shutting its petals for the night. The Inner Harbor shops at the trendy mall were all closed or closing. There was yellow crime scene tape around their WTC building, and armed men with rifles were guarding it. We couldn't even walk on that side of the street as we approached the Inner Harbor mall.

Where were we going to eat? It was now after noon, and I was hungry. The cop we asked directed us to Hooters, which had the distinction of being the only restaurant in Inner Harbor Baltimore operating on 9/11/01. So, hi-ho, hi-ho, off to Hooters we would go.

How surreal is it to be watching the airplane attack on the World Trade Center replaying, over and over on national television, while a jiggly blonde in tight, short shorts asks you for your order in Hooters-speak?

"What's wrong with this picture?" I asked Chris, my second-in-command, "President George W. Bush is exhorting the nation to remain calm, and I am ordering chicken wings from someone in microscopically tight shorts with the name Bambi on her name tag."

The conference limped to a conclusion, and I stayed up all night, brainstorming a way to "help." In line at the airport, where all of us were in the longest lines I have ever seen, attempting to arrange transport back to the Midwest, James Leach, then the ranking Republican on the House

Finance Committee and a Senator from Davenport (now Iowa City), Iowa, was in line ahead of us.

I extracted a promise from him that, if I could get my "Celebrate Citizenship" brainstorm off the ground, he would come and be the keynote speaker. I did, and he did.

After months of organizing, including securing the Glenview Middle School Band, which had just been voted the best middle school band in the state of Illinois, I held my Swan Song as a Sylvan owner. We rented the Pleasant Valley High School auditorium and held a fund-raiser, which was matched, dollar for dollar, by Sylvan. The proceeds were to go to the families of the victims of the WTC bombing, for their college education.

Andrea Zinga, the local WHBF Channel 4 newswoman signed on first. Then, the *Daily Dispatch* agreed to print thousands of flyers to publicize the event, which was to be held on November 11, Veteran's Day. This was exactly two months from the date of the attack. Senator Leach had five speaking engagements that day, but, true to his word, he agreed to come and speak as the final speaker of the evening.

"Happy" Joe Whitty, local pizza king, also spoke. Krystal Whitty, his daughter, was to sing. John Marx, columnist for the *Daily Dispatch* was another speaker, and Ryan Nolan of KWQC, Channel 6, was also featured. Interspersed with the professional speakers were original poems and essays written by our Sylvan students, and, in the lobby afterwards, we sold red, white and blue popcorn, patriotic pins, Krispy Kreme doughnuts and all manner of things for the cause. We raised over $1,000. Even the local funeral home contributed a guest book, for all of our students to sign and send on to New York City, and, as a final wonderful memory, Jim Weir, the director of Glenview's Band, received a surprise Channel 4 award as one of that station's honored teachers, as voted by his students. It was truly a great way to sign off after fifteen years as the owner of the Sylvan Learning Center, and to do some good, as well.

Hooters Story Number II:

In the fall semester of 2003, while teaching at one of the six local colleges in the area, Hooters once again became relevant. This was a class designed to prepare students to write resumés and go through interviews in the real world. I had gone to considerable time and effort to arrange for real interviewers from industry to come to my classroom to make the experience more realistic. One gentleman, in fact, worked part-time as an interviewer for Sedona, a part-time placement agency. Another gentleman had hired and fired at Deere & Company before retirement and yet another had done the same for Alcoa.

Prior to the actual interview date, one student, whom I shall refer to as Courtney because of her resemblance to "Friends" star Courtney Cox, asked me if she could interview for a position as a waitress at Hooters during her mock interview.

Initially, I was tempted to say no, which would have been a knee-jerk reaction to the name of the restaurant itself. Then, I thought about this girl's major: American Sign Language. When I had asked her what her career goals were, with a degree in ASL, she had said, "To get up on outta' here." She said that she assumed that she would have to move to a large city to find work as an ASL interpreter, and I concurred, saying that her other choice would be to complete her ASL degree and also obtain a teaching credential. When I asked her if she wanted to do this, and, therefore, wanted her interview to be with a potential school district employer, she had responded, "What do you think I am…crazy?"

She went on to say that children were not her goal in life…ever. It seemed that the prospect of working with them, full-time, had all the appeal of a root canal for Courtney.

Therefore, when Courtney asked me if she could interview for a position as a waitress at Hooters, knowing that her current jobs were as a waitress for Applebee's and as a weekend cocktail waitress on one of our Mississippi River gambling boats, I thought, "Who am I to interfere with her life's calling?" It appeared that waitressing was her immediate and future goal. Possibly her past, her present and her future. Therefore, I said that she could, indeed, interview to become a member of the crack Hooters wait staff.

She immediately countered with, "Can I wear something low-cut and plunging for the interview?"

I said that that did not seem like a good idea, and that she should dress as our text-book had advised: wear something that you would normally wear to church. Who knew that Courtney was a member of the Church of What's Happening Now!?

Since I knew that hearing the very word Hooters would cause a raised eyebrow or two, I made my husband call the male interviewer the night before.

"Larry, one of the girls you will be interviewing is going to be interviewing for a position at Hooters."

There is no record of his response. Later, he said he thought it was a joke.

I should mention here that Larry is not the kind of guy to get rattled easily. He has a loose personality, spent eight years in the Navy, and likes to tell a risqué joke as much as the next guy. I commented that he was the only one of our friends who did not wear underwear, and the person with whom I shared this fact said, "How do you know?"

I know because his wife told me, of course. I am taking it on faith, just as I hope that he has taken it on faith that I did NOT intentionally set him up for what was to occur on the fateful day of the mock interview. I had no idea that Courtney would behave as though there were no filter between her brain and her mouth.

The interview started with one of the ten questions I had distributed to the class in advance, to help them prepare, which was, "What do you consider your greatest asset?" These questions had been culled from the most-commonly asked questions in real-life job interviews. They should have been "safe."

The Hooters girl immediately answered enthusiastically, "I've got great boobs!" and came close to flashing us all.

The interview was turning in to the most surreal teaching day of a thirty-three year career. And I've had some pretty surreal teaching days!

This response caused Larry to redden noticeably. He shared later that now he didn't know exactly where to direct his gaze. Memories of his former days at Alcoa, complete with classes on sexual harassment and grounds for same were rushing to the forefront of his heated brain. He realized that he was treading on dangerous ground, if this were a real-world environment.

I had told my class that they were to score the interviews. Fortunately, this particular batch was not being filmed, although earlier ones had been. The class was sitting in the audience, and was told to pretend that there was an invisible Gardol shield separating them from the interviewer and the interviewee. However, the snickering had begun. Even though they were not to let on by remark or interaction that they were present, as, indeed, they were not supposed to *be* present, it was difficult for us all. There were categories for the class to score constituting "attire," "ability to sell one's self," "knowledge of the company" and "follow-up questions," among others.

The next question Larry asked was, "What do you consider your greatest weakness?"

"Probably my ass," said Courtney. Although she then lapsed in to some discussion of her abdominal muscles and other body parts that left us all gasping in a futile attempt to remain quiet, as instructed.

In the back of the room, I was finding this difficult myself and called out, "Larry: you're old enough to remember *Lost in Space*. Picture an alarm noise (Ka-Yu-Gah! Ka-Yu-Gah!) and a voice saying, 'Danger, Will Robinson! Danger!'"

Larry bravely continued, attempting to regain his equilibrium, although a tell-tale blush had crept up his usually pale white Swedish cheeks and neck. After determining that Courtney currently worked on a gambling boat on weekends as a cocktail waitress, he asked her, "Have you ever had anyone you were waiting on do or say something inappropriate when you were waiting on them? And how did you handle it?"

Courtney responded, in a very puzzled voice, "Like what?"

This put the onus of naming names and describing offenses clearly on Larry, who had already decided that he was skating on very thin ice.

He moved on, asking, "How did you get along with your supervisor on the Pair of Dice?" (fictitious name)

Courtney said, "Well, once, when I left to go to the rest room, he said to me, when I returned, in front of everybody, 'Either you sneaked outside to have a cigarette or you took one gigantic dump.'"

This disclosure seemed to leave the entire class gasping for air. T.M.I.—Too Much Information. I know it wasn't doing too much for me. I tried to figure out if any self-respecting executive in the entire state of Illinois would ever volunteer to "mock interview" members of my class again.

At this exact point, Courtney looked out at the assembled class members (through the Gardol shield) and said, "This interview isn't going too well, is it?"

Talk about your understatements.

Larry finally concluded the interview. I don't remember how. I doubt if he does, either. I do remember saying that everyone should be "pregnant" at the next class, when I meant to say "present," but, hey! It was that kind of moment. Larry and I collapsed in the hall outside the classroom in helpless mirth after the class had filed out. Larry said, "I think I need a shot of Jack Daniels." I needed an entire bottle of Jack Daniels.

Later, I read that Hooters has launched an airline and visions of Courtney flashing the passengers entered my head. I also saw the following Hooters item, which I shall report verbatim:

Dateline: Belleville, Illinois – Parents complained that Superintendent Darrel Hardt took junior high students to a Hooters restaurant during a school trip. Hardt said the chain restaurant was the only inexpensive place that would accommodate twenty-six students.

Others tell me that Hooters was the only restaurant that could accommodate the students without shepherding them across a busy freeway.

I would have been willing to chance it with the mock interview group, but apparently the Superintendent of Schools in Belleville, Illinois, was not.

WORDS

If fewer words were spoken,
If fewer words were said,
If deeds alone were the mark of a man.
Not the "catch" of an eloquent pledge.

If fewer words were spoken.
If fewer words were said,
If, for all the fake forensics,
There were simple words, instead.

And a man stated just what he started to state
Without false fuss or further ado.
If you weren't a politician,
I'd probably listen to you.

(*Written at age 16 and still true today.)

The author, at age sixteen, in 1961, when "Words" was composed.

True Tales of Child-Raising

(*These anecdotes were typed up and mailed as 1990's Christmas letter.)

Anecdote #1:

Stacey is very musical and loves to sing. They told us at pre-school that she "loves to sing loud." Not well, but loud. Ever since she was a tiny little girl, I have always sung "I Feel Pretty" from "West Side Story" to her as we dried off after her bath.

Imagine my surprise, when, on the line, "Who's that pretty girl in the mirror there? (What mirror, where?) Who can that attractive girl be?" I finally heard what she had been singing all this time.

"Who's that pretty girl in the mirror there? Who can that tractor girl be?"

With a Dad who put in 36 years with John Deere, if those weren't the *real* lyrics, for her, they should be.

Anecdote #2:

While driving across the "Mighty Mickey-ssippi," which is what three-year-old Stacey used to call the Mississippi river, I heard her singing along to that old tune "Hang on, Sloopy" and she was singing, "Hang on, Snoopy!"

When I corrected her, she changed it to, "Hang on, Stupid!"

Anecdote #3:

We enjoyed the phone call home from Stacey and Steve and Regina, who had gone to Chicago ("Cago" to Stacey). "Are you in Chicago?" Craig asked.

"No," she said, somewhat puzzled, "I'm in a hotel room."

Anecdote #4:

I was amused to see how puzzling our familiar idioms can be to foreigners.

I clearly remember my Swedish college student, Per Olof Gustaffsson, writing me from Duse Udde on Lake Vanerne in Sweden that it was "snowing cats and dogs."

I asked Stacey, innocently enough, "How do you like them apples?" one day, and she responded, quite seriously, "What apples, Mom?"

Anecdote #5:

When Scott, then age 3, observed a dead raccoon on the way home from his grandparents' house, he said, "That raccopoon was kicking my dad's car!" For some unknown reason, he then began calling the dead "raccopoon" Sparky.

Anecdote #6:

We were working hard to toilet-train son Scott and to get him to use "the potty," as he knew he should, rather than simply relieving himself in the great outdoors. But, you know how it is when, as his sister Stacey used to put it, "I'm pwetty busy pwaying."

One day during this time, he came in the house with a particularly guilty look on his face. Finally, unable to control himself and craving absolution, he burst out, "Nobody went potty over there by the swing set!"

Anecdote #7:

First sexual question, asked by Scott when age 3: "Mommy, does you got a tail?"

Anecdote #8:

Stacey has an active imagination. The other day she told me a very detailed story involving going to the moon.

She got to the moon on a rocket; it was cold there. So far, so good. When she arrived, she found Linda, Nelson and "Beff" were there, along with their dog, eating pickles and French fries.

I asked, "Was Neil Armstrong there?"

"No, Mom," she said, very exasperated with my denseness, "*Nelson!*"

Memories

I am reminded of the time that I attempted to do something nice for my Dad. It was spring, and I thought that he would be thrilled if I were to wash the car, unbidden.

He probably would have liked it, if I had not driven the car on to the very wet back yard lawn. As I hosed it off, the car proceeded to sink in to the lawn up to its hubcaps, although this escaped my attention at the time.

When I tried to drive it from the crime scene, things took a turn for the worse. I could not get the car out of the lawn.

I heard someone whistling as they walked by on the sidewalk below. It was Chet Schmitz, (an awesome whistler, who later played trombone professionally in a symphony orchestra), walking home. I summoned Chet and asked his advice, but he was convulsed with laughter. Which didn't help the situation at all.

Eventually, my father had to jack the car OUT of the lawn on 2x4's.

I also remember, as I was using an old Rex-Air that had a bottom level in to which you put water, vacuuming the inside of the car and pulling the thing too far over, so that water spilled over on to the electrical switch. I was being electrocuted. I couldn't let go of the vacuum, so I began yelling, as loudly as I could, hoping that my father would come help me. He was inside the kitchen, watching at the time.

Finally, I was able to pull my numb and tingling hand from the vacuum cleaner and went in the house, badly shaken.

"Didn't you hear me yelling?" I asked.

"Well, yes," he answered mildly, "but I just thought you were yelling at some friends."

I was once put in charge of another electrical appliance…in this case, an electric lawn-mower. My father thought it was a wonderful alternative to a gas mower, as you never had to start it. You merely had to plug it in and start it up.

You did, however, have to be careful that you didn't cut the cord, and, on hills, I was told, always mow DOWN, not UP.

I forgot this and the mower ran over my tennis shoe. All I could see was that my white Keds were turning red from blood. The mower had rolled over my foot. (DOWN, standing above it, not UP!)

I limped in to the house, where my sister and I removed what was left of my shoe, to discover that my toe was intact. Only my toe-nail was missing. Grim as that sounds, I have seldom felt luckier!

When I was in sixth grade, a bunch of us went to camp. I don't remember much about camp, other than that the cabins were bug-infested, dark and unpleasant. We had only bunk beds and communal showers and bathroom(s) and we had to walk a long way to get to them.

There was a dance at some point during "camp." I was wearing a chemise dress, then the style. Someone said it looked like a maternity dress; I was mortified and had a horrible time at the dance.

A tree had fallen on the trampoline.

Friend Beverley and I attempted to take a canoe out, but we couldn't agree on a direction and so the canoe overturned while we argued about whether to go this direction or that.

On the last day of camp, everyone was picked up by the Siessegers. I don't know why they left me there. I suspect that Jane didn't like me and just wanted to abandon me in this hell-hole.

I sat there on the metal edge of that crumpled and broken trampoline for hours, wondering how I was going to get home from Camp Wapsie-Y or whatever-the-hell it was called. It should have been called Camp Hellacious. It had been a truly horrible week in every respect, and now I was marooned there for life!

Finally, after it became clear that no one was ever coming to pick me up (all the other car-poolers having left with the Siessegers), I found a phone and called home. No one was there except for my sister, who was too young to drive.

I ended up having to ride home with the camp counselor. To this day, the word "camp" does not summon good memories. Later, I watched this very same counselor, during a Four-H activity night, host a balloon-blowing contest that ended with him passing out face-first on to a concrete floor and knocking out two front teeth. Why that particular detail sticks with me, I do not know. Let's just say that having a balloon blowing-up contest is no longer on the list of sanctioned 4-H activities.

My husband, Craig, and I, serious golfers, about to embark on another golf adventure.

Six Golf Stories For the Ages

I once had a fellow working at a golf course tell me that I "ought to write a book" about my golfing experiences. I don't know if writing an entire book is merited, but I do think that my experiences while golfing are worth mentioning. So, here are six unrelated incidents. Make of them what you will.

Story Number One:

My first introduction to golf came when my mother decided, when I was in the sixth grade, that she was going to hire the coach of our local golf team to teach Candy Hatfield and me to golf. It was summertime, and Coach Duvall, who had had a state championship golf team in the state the preceding year, was willing, if not eager, to take on the instruction of two twelve-year old girls who had never played the game.

I should mention, first, that my mother's clubs were genuine antiques. They were all old and tweedy-looking, with little spirals of wire sticking out from where they were wrapped around the heads of these things. I was totally embarrassed to have to play with anything that looked this bad. And the bag was worse.

To counteract the image created by the really crappy golf clubs, I wore my new blue suede shoes. These were definitely cool. The song had just come out (OK, so I'm dating myself; what do I care?) and I had these really nifty

70

blue slip-on shoes. They were comfortable, too, which was good, since Candy and I didn't have a ride to the country club and were going to have to walk there over a long, winding, gravel road.

I always got the feeling that Mr. Duvall was not really all that enthused about playing golf with a couple of twelve-year old girls who happened to be teachers' kids. Why would I get that impression? Oh, I don't know. Maybe because all we ever did was chip and putt. No REAL playing, just chipping and putting on the hole closest to the winding gravel road. This particular hole placement will soon become important in my story.

It was while chipping and putting and putting and chipping…especially the chipping….that, not knowing my own strength, I hit one that soared out on to the road and knocked the back window out of a passing pick-up truck. There was a screech of tires and the bewildered driver made a bee-line for us.

Mr. Duvall never let me forget about the broken-window-in-the-truck incident. Of course, my family had to pay for the broken window. It became a giant family joke.

However, the worst of those ill-fated lessons at age twelve was yet to come. When Candy and I completed our day's lesson and returned to the clubhouse, hot and tired in the July heat, I took off my new blue suede shoes, put them in my golf bag, and went inside. We got a pop (Orange Nehi, if I remember correctly). When we returned to the spot on the sidewalk outside the clubhouse where my golf bag still sat forlornly in its pull cart, my shoes were gone. To this day, I don't know who took them or why. I DO know that walking home five miles, barefoot, over a gravel road does nothing to instill a love of the game of golf in the neophyte player.

Story Number Two:

Later, I returned to play the Independence course as a young bride. It was the Fourth of July weekend. It was hotter than the proverbial pistol. I had not played golf since the ill-fated lessons with Candy. My husband, an accomplished golfer, thought it would be a good idea for us to take up the game as a couple. I was less sure, but willing to give it a go at the club to which my parents belonged.

The game was really going poorly. I still think that golf should be a seven-hole sport. Seven holes is about right. Nine holes is too long and eighteen holes is like the Bataan Death March. I have never been able to hit a golf ball with a three of anything, and, at this point in my golfing career, no one had seen fit to inform me of the existence of the five-wood or other more useful clubs. I was still in the mode where I might as well have been issued a large bat, which I could use to just pound golf balls in to the surface of the course. God knows I couldn't hit anything up in the air with a three (wood or iron, makes no difference) and yet I had been told that this was the club of choice for the fairway. So I soldiered manfully (or womanfully) along, driving golf ball after golf ball about 3 feet, and hitting it yet again.

After seven holes of this foolishness in blazing heat, I was ready to quit. And, apparently, so was my husband, if you can believe that. (And I know that you can.) Is there anything worse than being a good golfer saddled with someone who has to hit it ten times to go one hundred yards? I ask this rhetorical question having just returned from playing golf with four golfers, one of whom, I later learned, has Alzheimer's. This went a long way towards explaining why that particular player kept wandering over to lakes and bushes and "panning for balls," when she should have been hitting her own ball.

I talked my husband in to quitting after the seventh hole in Independence, which ended up back near the row of cabins leading in to the golf club. It wasn't really that difficult. It was hot. I was horrible. We headed toward the gravel road entrance that went right past the cabins where some of the town's residents lived during the summer.

It was then that we became aware of a crowd that had gathered in front of the third cabin on the left-hand side of the gravel road leading to the clubhouse. An ambulance was parked in front of the cabin and a very exhausted nurse was shouting, "Does anyone here know CPR?"

My husband and I had just completed a CPR course at Illini Hospital in Silvis, Illinois. We had all pumped the chest of Resusci-Annie and learned about establishing airways and compressions and all the rest of it. This was because my father-in-law had had one major coronary and we wanted to "be prepared." I was carrying the "reminder" card as to procedure in my purse and I immediately got it out. The exhausted good Samaritan, the nurse who had been administering CPR to Frank Barger, was only too happy to hand off to new volunteers when she heard "We know CPR." The victim, Frank Barger, was Trudy Barger's dad. I knew Trudy slightly from high school.

Thus began Mr. Toad's Wild Ride in the Independence ambulance. Why they sent the ambulance out with just a driver is a very good question, which I will have to ask someone some day. Mr. Barger, who was the usher and ticket-taker at the town movie theater, had been wallpapering at the nearby cabin when he was felled by a heart attack. The nurse next door had already established an airway and "bagged" the victim. She had begun CPR, but, as anyone who has ever done CPR knows firsthand, it is an exhausting procedure. One person, alone, is soon worn out.

"Get in the ambulance!"

There was no turning back now!

And so it began.

One compression, followed by a curve in the road. One of us would fly into the side of the ambulance while the other attempted to compress Mr. Barger's chest, as we had learned to do. I felt like a piece of popcorn inside a popper.

Mr. Barger did not look good. Much as I would have liked to help Trudy's dad, he was blue when we started working on him. I doubt if he ever had a fighting chance.

When we reached the ambulance garage, the attendants rushed to his aid. He was wheeled in to the ambulance on a gurney. No one thought to turn off the ambulance siren, which blared loudly and ricocheted off the walls of the ambulance garage. Finally, practically deafened by the noise, I climbed over the partition dividing the back area from the driver's seat and began fiddling with dials until I located the right one.

I followed the gurney in to the hospital and tried to find out if Mr. Barger had a chance. He had once kicked me out of "Jack the Ripper" for sneaking in the back door from the alley without paying, but I bore him no ill will.

Alas, although a sinus rhythm was established, Mr. Barger could not be saved. And thus my love of the game of golf grew by leaps and bounds.

Story Number Three:

On our next golf outing, sponsored by a local tavern owned by a friend, a small ground squirrel was found, dead, near my ball. It appeared that I might have hit and killed him. To this day, I maintain that the beer truck ran over him. The cow that I hit between the eyes in a field across the fence from the Independence course, fared better. He lived to tell his herd-mates about my poor aim.

I was forced in to retirement for many years. Some would say not as many as necessary, but those are the nay-sayers among us. I did not play golf again for many years.

Story Number Four:

It was not until May of 1996 that my husband and I joined Short Hills Country Club in East Moline, Illinois. I wanted to join for the social aspects, but my husband really likes to play golf, which must be because he can play well. I, on the other hand, was still beating balls in to the ground with various golf implements. I never met a divot I didn't like.

We were enticed in to joining by friends who were members. They invited us to play in a six-some in the All-You-Can-Eat Shrimp Boil. In return for pretending to be a golfer during a two-ball event that featured six-member teams playing best ball, I would be rewarded with all the shrimp I could eat. It was too good an offer to pass up. My husband and I said, "Sign us up!"

The night of the event it was pouring down rain. There were three carts. I was partnered with a gentleman whom I shall call Bob. We had the only cart without a roof, so, of course, we got soaked throughout our playing time, while the other two couples remained relatively dry.

From the outset, there were several incidents that did not bode well for our team. For one thing, as our cart drove up the very first incline, my clubs fell off and the cart behind us ran over them. The clubs had not been properly secured by the caddies.

Second, Bob thought that a couple on the first hole we reached was "just practicing" and went out on to the green, threw down his ball, and began taking practice putts. I was in awe. I thought that these people were, indeed, playing for real in the All You Can Eat Shrimp Boil Two-ball, and, as it turns out, I was right. Bob had just committed a heinous faux pas.

Third, our team, (never really much in to reading the rules), was teeing off pretty randomly when a guy in another cart came racing over to inform us that it was "women on odd," "men on even."

Unfortunately, as he approached us at warp speed, he could not brake quickly enough, and, in addition to running over Bob's wife's foot, he tore up about 30 feet of the fairway when his cart brakes apparently locked. Later, my brother-in-law became very concerned, as this was "his" hole to police, and it now had a huge skid mark that needed re-sodding.

We limped back to the clubhouse in the rain, where I stood in line a long time to use the sole hairdryer. I looked like a drowned rat. Finally, I had my turn. I dried my golden locks. When I looked halfway normal, I went upstairs to claim the all-you-can-eat shrimp, only to learn that (a) everyone on my team of six except me had already finished eating (b) they were now in the bar (c) all the shrimp were gone.

Story Number Five:

In order to further improve my very rusty golf game, I also joined an EWG (Executive Women's Golf League) about this same time. This league met at a very long and very narrow course that I have been told is one of the most difficult courses in this area. Who knew? All I know is that I never broke seventy (for nine holes) at this course, hold the record for getting caught in the automatic sprinkler, and frequently had to shoot in to a crowd of deer.

Glynn's Creek, the course in question, has long had a problem with deer, who have become so tame that they will come right up to you, during your shot, and eat the bark off a nearby tree. It's as though they want to taunt you by saying, "Hey, loser! Look at me! I can eat the bark off this tree and you can't do anything about it!"

I once shot in to an entire family of four deer: Mommy, Daddy, Bambi I and Bambi II.

The reason I was always getting caught in the sprinkler system at Glynn's Creek is that we teed off at 5:00 p.m. By the time Jane (my partner) and I made it to the ninth hole, it was getting dark. This was because we took about twenty strokes apiece per hole.

The sprinkler system would kick in, automatically, because it was dusk. Jane was even worse than me, which I did not think was possible. I don't think she will be mad at me for saying this. If she is, then I take it back and offer my apologies.

My handicap at this time was thirty-six, the very highest possible for nine holes. I had nowhere to go but up.

My friend Judy, who had had one lesson from a very good pro at Glynn's Creek named Kurt Schnell, recommended that I take a lesson from him. She said that he was expensive, but well worth the money. I certainly couldn't get any worse, as I was basically just pounding golf balls into the fairway with my three-wood, harming small animals, and getting wet while playing. I also had developed one hell of a slice.

I signed up for a lesson with Mr. Schnell. He was a very good teacher, who used both verbal instruction, pictures, and a video-camera, to actually film me in action. Mr. Schnell gave me one lesson, laughed a great deal, and, soon thereafter, moved to Omaha, where he is a golf pro to this day. If quizzed, he would be able to testify that I have the worst form of any female golfer he has ever seen. I do everything wrong. I bend my arm when I hit the ball. I was slicing it to the right in a lovely arcing motion that was doing nothing to lower my thirty-six handicap. There is no proof to the rumor, however, that he moved to Omaha because he saw me play.

The first thing Mr. Schnell mentioned was, "You're holding the club all wrong."

He instructed me in the basic "Hello, Mr. Club" hand-shaking grip, which I still use today. If I have not said, "Hello, Mr. Club," I have not addressed the ball, and it will, for sure, soar directly in to the nearest right-hand sand trap or tree. Always right. Never left. Since I am playing with a Herky the Hawk ball currently, I have modified this to "Hello, Mr. Herky." As soon as I shoot Herky in to a lake on the right, I will go back to "Hello, Mr. Club."

With one lesson, a video-camera and plenty of laughter, Mr. Schnell was able to lower my handicap to twenty-three. Fine by me. I did not aspire to be better than that. But I still was frustrated by my lack of consistency. It was typical for me to hit 9-6-9-5-9-4 and so on. I could even par a hole or two, on occasion. But the next hole would be an eight or a nine.

My long game improved, but my short game did not. This may be because I was using the Purple Putter of Death, on the grounds that it matched my clubs, which were Blue Light Specials from K-Mart. The K-Mart clubs were about the weight of a tire iron, at least twenty years old, and totally ineffectual. They would be good if you were being attacked in the parking lot by gang members. On an actual golf course, they were a liability, rather than an asset.

I invested in some new clubs, new irons and a new putter, an Omega, as recommended by the EWG women's clinic staff. This did nothing to improve my putting, but I felt better about myself. At least I was stylish! I also liked the name: Omega. If there is a club called Alpha, I will purchase it.

Story Number Six:

The first club purchase, however, that literally changed my life and my game forever was a five-wood that I purchased at Sam's Wholesale Club. I bought it the night before the Ladies Invitational Member/Guest event. Everyone had told me what a great event this was, and how you could invite a guest to play for a pittance. There was a lunch. Nobody mentioned that the event was EIGHTEEN HOLES LONG and that almost everyone who participated was a real golfer who was at least sixty-five years of age. I think it was some sort of rule that you had to have blue hair.

Now, I do not like doing anything before 10:00 a.m., and the tee-off time was 9:00 a.m. I set my alarm clock, so that I would be up when my friend Judy picked me up, but I set it (accidentally) for 9:00 p.m., not 9:00 a.m.

Therefore, when Judy arrived at my door, all cheery and ready to go, I was still in my pajamas. I was neither cheery nor ready. My brand-new still shrink-wrapped club was ready, however, and in a nano-second, we were off, attempting to make it to the club before the tee-off time.

We did not quite make the tee-off time. We were late. We had to find "Number Three Hole" to join the group (our foursome) that had just left without us. I had no idea where the Number Three Hole was, so this complicated matters. I had always just ridden along in the cart, enjoying the great out-of-doors and the woodland creatures. We probably looked like a female version of Dumb and Dumber as we randomly tried out various holes to see if they were "three."

Eventually, we found Hole Number Three, however, and, indeed, our fellow two-some had already driven and were in mid-fairway. They were gracious enough to allow us to tee up and join them. I stepped up, removed the shrink wrap from my new Big Bertha, said, "Hello, Mr. Club" (I was not yet using Herky). Not having anywhere to discard the shrink wrap I had just removed from my club, I slapped it firmly on my butt. My partner almost cardiac arrested.

As I recall, she said, "You mean you have never played with that club before now?"

I said, "Of course not. If I had, would it still have the shrink wrap on it?"

Well, friends and neighbors, I want to let you know that a five-wood is the name of the game if you are a female golfer who cannot hit a three-wood to save her life. (Or anyone else's, judging from our unfortunate experience with Mr. Barger of Story One).

Now, I began the usual "hack and run" motif, where I hit it at least six or seven times to get to the edge of the green. At this point, one of the blue-haired golfers drove her cart up to us, all in a lather, and said, "If you hit it more than seven times, pick it up!"

I responded, "Lady, if I pick it up after only seven strokes I won't ever get to finish a hole."

She then hissed, "Read the rules! Read the rules!"

Finding this amusing and in a cavalier and fey barely-awake mood, I said, "Rules? Rules? We don't need no steenking rules."

This did not seem to amuse Ms. Blue Hair.

We continued our play.

Suddenly, the first nine, which had taken a very long time, indeed, to complete, was over. Quelle horror! This ordeal was supposed to last for ANOTHER nine holes. I said, "Judy, looks like we will be eating lunch somewhere else," turned the cart around, and we left.

To this day, I have not played in another Member/Guest function. I'm still out there practicing, however, so small animals: beware!

Neither a Twiner Nor a Purrer Be

When I was in college, I gave my parents a Siamese cat, which they named Sam. Sam was an ornery critter. I remember my journey to pick him out. I thought it was cute that he hid under a chair, only occasionally reaching out to take a swipe at passersby. I did not know that this might signal a personality disorder of the First Magnitude.

The first thing Sam did when he reached his new home was hide in a woodpile for a week. It wasn't even our woodpile! My parents took one look at this cat, a blue-tip Siamese with papers which had cost me a pretty penny, and promptly gave it away. But I turned the traditional legacy of parents to children, guilt ("the gift that keeps on giving") around and convinced them that Sam should be allowed to stay. It took Rick Roehrkasse, his temporary owner, about three days to get Sam out of the woodpile and return him to my parents.

As a pet, you want a cat that endears himself to you, twining through your legs in the kitchen upon your return from work or jumping into your lap to be petted and scratched before a roaring fire, purring contentedly. Sam seemed to have adopted the maxim, "Neither a twiner nor a purrer be."

Next time I get a cat, I will put out a job description first. The cats I have owned prefer hiding in woodpiles or furnaces, emitting inhuman noises that are grating to the ear, and breaking things. None of my cats even "meowed" in the traditional sense of the word. They all sounded like Mingo from the planet Mercury.

One night, Sam began yowling from the basement bedroom in the wee hours of the morning. There was a clothes chute that went directly from my parents' bedroom to the basement where Sam slept at night. Finally, Dad had had enough! He decided to try a little behavior modification.

Dad attached a long clothesline to Sam's collar. Every time Sam let out with a blood-curdling yowl, Dad yanked on the cord. Picture my father, lying there in bed, yanking away like a crazed weasel. Cruel as it may sound, the alternative, at this point, for Sam was a trip to the vet and the ultimate trip to Paw Print Gardens, that cemetery for deceased felines.

When Dad went to the basement to release Sam the next morning, he shot out of that basement as though he were jet-propelled! Right behind him was the foreign cat interloper that had *really* been making all this noise. Cat Number Two had apparently climbed in through the basement window and had been hiding behind the furnace. Dad had been jerking the wrong cat's chain all night long! (Insert your own "yanking your chain" joke here.)

Sam had always been cross-eyed, a characteristic of the breed, but you can bet that *this* morning, he was more cross than cross-eyed!

The Olympics

I had a rather unique experience this summer. After watching one-half of the 1984 Olympics on television in the United States, right through Mary Lou Retten's vaulting medal, I watched the last half on television in West Germany, Sweden, Denmark and Norway.

One obvious problem with watching a program broadcast in not one, but four languages I do not speak, was my inability to understand what the expert commentators were trying to say.

A race is still a race, after all, though, and, after reading some scathing British commentary in the London press about our United States coverage by ABC, I wasn't sure I had missed that much.

British columnist Julian Barnes, who specializes in television criticism for the *London Daily Mail*, wrote an article in which he reported experiences similar to my own, as he had watched the first half of the Olympics in Texas, on American television (ABC) and the second half of the competition in London on the BBC.

Among criticisms leveled at ABC's announcers and reporters, he described veteran anchorman Jim McKay as "a stumbling, blue-jacketed droner" and denounced the American athletes used as commentators, who, he said, fell short of their task by "letting out Apache war whoops as their sole analytic comment on a compatriot's performance." Ah, those wacky Brits!

Barnes was properly aghast at the ABC commentator who solemnly informed us, as one bicyclist closely tailed another, "The one who's not in front is breaking a lot of wind." He also didn't think much of John Williams' "Olympic Anthem." His exact words were, 'If you find the 'Chariots of Fire' theme moany and obvious, you haven't been subjected to John Williams' 'Olympic Anthem' 24 times or so an hour, before and after each commercial break."

Barnes hated the opening ceremony. "BBC viewers, unlike ABC viewers, were spared the ABC subtitles during the opening march past of contestants, which explained the size and location of each competing country. Not just with Bhutan ('location: Central Asia; size: approximately ½ Indiana') but with Belgium ('in NW Europe') and Bangladesh ('approximately the size of Wisconsin.')." Harsh words from this British critic! We might also say, "Them's fightin' words", which, as I recall, Americans did say to the British, circa 1776, with interesting results.

But let me return to my original topic and tell you what it was like watching the Olympics on foreign soil. The question, "How long can you tread water?" might be rephrased as, "How long can you watch the Swedish two-woman kayak races?" Or, the West German women's fencing team? The event that seemed to be of the most interest to these viewers was the celebrated decathlon duel between West Germany's Jurgen Hingsen ("the German Hercules") and Britain's Daley Thompson, which Thompson won. That is what I saw, and that is *all* I saw.

Carl Lewis was strictly, "Carl who?" in Denmark. I saw re-runs of the West German women's fencers taking the gold and falling over backwards in happiness afterwards fully seven times in one hour, on television in Munich. After a few evenings which consisted solely of watching obscure events won by the Danes, Germans, Swedes and

Norweigans, I was glad to be able to switch to "From Here to Eternity" and James Dean in "Rebel Without a Cause, even though both were dubbed in German, which I do not speak or understand. Still, it was an improvement. I was reminded of the time that my husband had said I would be a perfect candidate for the "Forward 100-Meter Roll," which, for all I know, is a real event.

Perhaps the attitude of Europeans I encountered was best summed up by my former Swedish student at Augustana College, Per Olof Gustaffsson, who flipped off his set in the middle of yet another cranking out of "Oh Say Can You See?" saying good-naturedly, "U.S. smashes the rest of the word. Bo-ring!"

To this American and many others, it was NOT boring. There is a resurgence of patriotism abroad in our land. The United States had a fantastic Olympics and, at the risk of being proclaimed an ugly American, I'm not afraid to tell the world.

However, I still could be amused by critics like Julian Barnes, and I enjoyed this anecdote he told, praising a British broadcaster named David Coleman.

"The games did throw up a few jollies. My favorite moment came at some eyelid-dropping time on Tuesday morning, when an American girl won the 400 meters. The habitual mayhem ensued, 'And there she is in the arms of her boyfriend,' exclaimed BBC sportscaster David Coleman warmly." (The incident referred to happened when Valerie Brisco-Hooks embraced her husband, Alvin Sr., after winning the Women's 400-meter race).

Coleman continued: "But by then the camera had panned across to the embrace. The man was lying splay-legged on his back and the gold medallist herself was atop him in what is usually referred to as the female missionary position. After a few moments, they rolled over and showed us the other way."

Coleman, understandably stumped for words, lunged for his mental fact file on the winner. What he came up with was this, "And she's got a 2-year-old son, Alvin Jr.!"

Concluded Barnes (on Coleman), "I shouldn't think a viewer in this land was at all surprised."

Query

Where's the me that used to be?
Where did this person go?
When did me become just we?
These answers I don't know.

It seems, in moving through my life,
I've ceased to be a "me."
Quit existing on my own terms
But only as a "we."

This anonymous identity
That fate's assigned me here
Does not promote tranquility
But makes me crazed, I fear.

I want a "me" before I die
I want to taste of "free."
So, where's the me that used to be?
I'm missing: tell me why?

11/26/96

Connie Corcoran Wilson

SAFE SEX?

From Monmouth, Illinois, we have the story of a Galesburg man who crossed the center line and crashed head-on into an oncoming truck, killing his female companion.

Sonny S. Martin, age 32, was found guilty on May 9, 2003, of aggravated driving under the influence. His female companion, Christina Vallerio, who was killed in the January 17, 2002, accident, was found with the steering wheel embedded in her back, naked from the waist down. The two had been driving from Scooters Cabaret, a strip club in Gladstone, Illinois, to their home in Galesburg. Although the two were not "dating," they had been living together with Mr. Morris's ex-wife. Mr. Morris was found outside the 1990 Chevy Caprice, his pants and underwear down around his ankles, wearing a condom.

Here's the part I don't get: the guy is using a condom. Usually, this is a sign of "safe sex." However, while he is having sex, Mr. Morris is hurtling 60 to 65 miles per hour down U.S. Highway 34, between Biggsville (no pun intended), in Henderson County, and Kirkwood, in Warren County (Illinois). Is this "safe sex" or a bizarre version of some sort of sexual demolition derby?

James Mueller, a truck driver for Sara Lee Bread Company, was following "about 12 to 15 car lengths" behind Mr. Morris, and described the Chevy Caprice as "driving erratically."

I would think so. I'm still trying to figure out how he was driving at all! Mr. Mueller, one of the eye-witnesses at the trial, described the Morris car as reaching speeds of 60 to 65 miles per hour and then dropping back to 30 to 35 miles per hour.

The Caprice crossed the centerline and hit a 1999 Freightline truck nearly head-on about 5:20 a.m., four miles east of the Henderson County line.

I served on two coroner's juries in Rock Island County in Illinois. Unlike other states, in Illinois a jury of regular folk like me have to decide whether a person involved in a fatal accident is guilty of several charges. If the death is ruled a "homicide" or "accidental" or if negligence is found by the jury, it can make a big difference in whether insurance pays off to the family.

Reckless homicide was one of the charges dropped in Mr. Morris's case, when the state failed to prove its case that he was high on marijuana at the time of the accident. Although Mr. Morris's blood alcohol level was .06, (below the legally intoxicated limit of .08 in Illinois), there was evidence of THC, a component of cannabis, in his urine.

Let's all keep in mind, while driving, that the person driving the other car might be Sonny Morris. And we know what that means.

DJ and RON

In my travels on the internet since 1995, I emerged as the comic relief in various chat rooms. During the years when my daughter was attending a Catholic elementary school, in the morning I found myself in CarChat while waiting for her to get ready for school. That is where I met DJ and Ron.

How or why I ended up in CarChat I cannot explain. It might stem from the time my car caught fire while I was waiting to be served at the McDonald's Drive-Up window in Coralville, Iowa. (You haven't lived until someone has tapped on your window and uttered the words, "Hey, lady! Your car is on fire!")

It might be that I was looking for someone with whom to share the term "McDent." (This is what you get when you shear off your driver's side mirror by making contact with the McDonald's drive-through window).

CarChat introduced me to two people with lives far more interesting than my own. By way of introducing a couple of the poems that otherwise would die with Ron, I want to give you this background on these guys.

DJ and Ron were friends from way back. They met in college at the University of Idaho in the early sixties and enlisted in the Air Force together during the Viet Nam War about the time that high school picture of me as a junior was taken: 1961. To hear DJ tell it, they just got up from their studies in the library and enlisted. Both were gear-heads (that is, they liked to work on cars) and both were pilots. DJ, in fact, was so good that he was chosen to train other U.S. helicopter pilots. Later, Dennis would find duty as a flight instructor for the Vietnamese that we were then "advising." One or both of them were, at one time, considered for astronaut training. DJ liked Roy Orbison; Ron was a closet Elvis freak.

My life seemed boring and ordinary talking to DJ and Ron. To hear tales of derring-do, past and present, from these two was quite something. Ron, however, said, "I cannot imagine the gamut of emotions that you must pass through every week: kids, husband, life, work, friends, allegiances, affiliations, business. Compared to yours, my life is a fairly simple structure." I doubted that, but those were his words.

Ron, whose screenname was "Ratstuf" (changed from RatShit, his Air Force name) was the star of the CarChat room. Others respected him for his obvious expertise, his fleet of Cobra cars, gathered over years of car collecting, his knowledge of all things mechanical.

Ron thought I was "a female version of DJ," his best friend. This was indeed high praise, as DJ was one of the brightest and wittiest people I ever encountered online.

In high school, Ron had played basketball, baseball and football, but, as he said, "It was just a small enough school that, if you weren't wheelchair-bound, you needed to play something." He said he had been on student council in his sophomore year, but shied away from anything but working on cars in his last years of high school. I think the town was Wenatchee, Washington, but Ron was always vague as to his exact location, an occupational necessity when you testify in court for the DEA (Drug Enforcement Agency) against drug king-pins.

In his final year of high school, Ron's parents were killed in a car accident. They were on their way back from a golf event. He told me, "The couple of weeks after my folks were killed were very weird. I continued to stay at the house for the next couple of days, and, although I had no immediate family in town, my dad's attorney and his wife, who were also good personal friends of my folks, invited me to stay with them until school was out in two months. I declined, of course. Tough guy, you know. After some arrangement was made for funds to keep me going until legal stuff was out of the way, I just sort of drifted through that time period. Even my girlfriend's folks offered to let me stay in their basement until I could figure out what to do. Everyone was just great during this time period. I felt pretty well buoyed up by all the concern, I guess.

My dad's brother only stayed in town for a week after the services, until the will was read. My folks, had, of course, not anticipated such an early demise. At least not for both of them. There was no guardian specified, and they really had not made much provision for distribution of assets beyond the standard legalese. As their closest living relative, everything that was not specifically designed to go to someone else (Dad had one brother; Mom had two sisters) remained with me.

My uncle got a hotel room in town. This did not thrill him much, as he lived in San Jose, California. None of them made it to the services. I could write a whole story just covering that and the next six months.

I was already enrolled at the University of Idaho. I saw no reason to change my plans. Nor did I even feel capable of making any other arrangements.

After graduation, I put in my last summer working at the warehouse that had been my summer job since I was thirteen. The folks had left me their cabin at Lake Chelan, so the attorney sold the folks' house for me, and I moved up there until I took off for school.

I met DJ at school. He was a year ahead of me. He had taken a few years off to work before succumbing to his parents' demands for higher education. We met over the hoods of our respective cars and found some channels of similar interest."

I never met Ron "in the flesh." He was always just words and ideas on a screen, but what fascinating words they were. After he died, I felt like, some day, I wanted to put the few poems he had shared with me down on paper, permanently, and this is that opportunity.

After serving in Viet Nam, Ron had gone to work for the DEA (Drug Enforcement Agency), flying drug interception raids off the coasts of Florida and Texas. He would use AOL to keep in touch with "the office." He sometimes sent exciting tales of his day's "work." My days seemed very "blah" and boring by comparison. Ron was the oldest flying Marshall in the U.S. The powers-that-be were attempting to force him out of the cockpit, though, and would eventually succeed. He would first be run over at a road-block and, while in the hospital for the broken leg he had incurred, the tumor on his optic nerve would be discovered. This tumor would eventually kill him.

DJ's family more-or-less adopted Ron when they became college friends and invited him to come to their home for all holidays. As DJ said, "You need to keep in mind that, notwithstanding my folks adopting Ron, he pretty much raised himself through late adolescence and into and beyond adulthood. I know that I represent one of the steadying influences in his life. We have discussed this at length. He tends to do wild things, but returns to the nest periodically for a reality check. (The nest being wherever I am.) I don't take this lightly. He is not a kid and certainly does not act like one, but, because there were no constraints placed on him past age eighteen, he pretty much did whatever he pleased. And still does. This does not always work out favorably, and his consternation at why it didn't is the subject of many of our conversations.

When we were in college and in the Air Force, and even now, I think, I was always the dominant personality and some of the things he did were more to establish that he had some independence. My observation is that, like many people, he needed constant input, approval and discipline in order to determine how he should behave. I think I served as his surrogate mentor or sensei (Japanese for teacher/mentor/guide). Without a Mom or Dad to check with, he just sort of formed his own credo to live by.

I am slightly older than Ron, of course, and this gap was much more noticeable in our younger years in college and the service. He joined the Air Force with me, mostly because I don't think that he wanted to stay in school if I wasn't going to be there. I had some overwhelming attack of Jingoism at the onset of the Viet Nam conflict. Plus, I was just sort of idling through school with absolutely no idea of what I intended to do for my life's work when I graduated. (*Editor's note: DJ would later follow his father in to banking as a career, although he said he had NO such intention at this time.)

When I announced my intention to leave school and join the Air Force, there was no discussion. Ron, in effect, slammed his books shut and said, 'Let's go!' We were pretty young and impetuous and it 'seemed like a good idea at the time.'

As we were not college graduates, we got to go through OCS (Officer Candidate School), which still results in a commission but takes a bit longer. Many in our group did not make it to the end. As we were both licensed pilots, we joined with the idea that we would become fighter pilots, but the lack of a diploma worked against us. The other requirement for jets was that you make a six-year commitment. That was out of the question for us. We wanted to start flying immediately. They offered us transport assignments and assured us that this was as worthy a job as zooming around the skies with our silk scarves trailing out of the cockpits. With no real viable alternatives, we acquiesced and were sent off to flight school at Chanute Air Force Base in Rantoul, Illinois.

About halfway through four-engine school, the Air Force decided I had absorbed all I needed and qualified me at that time, while simultaneously asking me to be an instructor for the next two months. I agreed, but bargained with them for their promise to send me to helicopter flight school. The deal was struck, and, when I announced my good fortune to Ron, he was virtually terror-struck. Up to this point, we had done everything as a dynamic duo, at least as far as school and the Air Force were concerned.

The situation now was that I would only be there for two more months, and then I would be sent off to North Dakota for rotorcraft school. Ron, on the other hand, would be sent somewhere else, probably Viet Nam. This did not set well with him, and some serious discussion ensued over the next few weeks. I was perplexed as to why he would feel I was abandoning him, but he did.

Following graduation from multi-transport training, Ron was sent out to Pleiku. I headed for the flat country of North

Dakota. Six months of seriously intense training resulted in my graduation at the head of the class. Thirty-two guys started; twenty finished. I was offered their version of a 'plum' assignment: flight instructor at Tan Son Nhut Air Force Base in Saigon, training the ARVN (Army of the Republic of Viet Nam) pilots. Ron and I had sporadically communicated. He was having a reasonably good time flying troops and freight from zone to zone, getting shot at, and pretty much leading an exciting life, while I had been instructing pilots state-side.

I wrote to Ron and told him I was coming to Saigon; maybe we could try to get together. We are talking some serious distances here. You don't just check out a plane and go visit your buddies.

I had a great time being the acknowledged expert on things that leave the ground to a bunch of fellows who, up until six years ago, had been working in rice fields. These guys were selected to go to prep school in Viet Nam. Then, upon graduation, they were sent to the United States to college. Then they were sent back home to serve in the military. The U.S. goal, of course, was to turn the war over to the ARVN after appropriate training. That never really transpired, but we sure processed a ton of helicopter pilots!

Teaching people to fly a helicopter....people that had never even driven a car until they were twenty, much less looked under the hood...was an exercise in itself. Helicopters are very complex aircraft. They require a great deal of coordination and every control input requires an accommodation in some other area. Depress the left pedal and you need to compensate with a deft twitch of the cyclic stick. Move the cyclic back and you need to increase power with the collective. Blah, blah, blah. By and large, you pretty much need to be able to become part of the craft. It is much easier if you were raised around mechanical things and have had some experience working on them, so that you can envision how all the linkages work together. Most guys that have swapped transmissions or two, or installed tri-power on their Chevy V8 learn to fly quite readily. The bulk of these guys just never 'got' it. It was quite frustrating for me, the teacher.

After my original six-month stint as an instructor, I requested a transfer back to multi-engine planes and an assignment to a forward base, preferably Pleiku or near there. I got what I wanted and wound up in the 606th Air Commando Squadron with Ron (Ratshit). We were flying 'candlestick' missions at night out of Pleiku. It was very different from an 8-to-5 job back in Saigon. I will not bore you with tales of derring-do. All I can say is that the others told me that Rat (Ron) was very glad to see me, and the others indicated that his mood changed dramatically with my arrival."

I met DJ in person in Las Vegas for lunch. He came to the hotel where my husband and son and I were staying (Paris) and took me to lunch at Mon Ami Gabi. It was a five-hour lunch, during which the bets I had made at the Sports Book, where my son and husband held forth after meeting him, came in, for me, while their bets tanked.

I took much of the accumulated correspondence from the years I had spent talking to Ron with me and gave copies to DJ. Many were about their friendship, which ended abruptly with Ron's death from that inoperable brain tumor, on a Christmas Eve which I am remembering as having been 1999 or 2000. I ran in to DJ that night, online, sitting in a hangar that housed Ron's classic cars, and he was pretty wasted. He had flown to Washington state to help the widow with arrangements, and I am sure he was a great comfort to her during this time of trouble.

Ron wrote me, in one e-mail, "DJ has a bunch of photos and albums spread out all over the place. If nothing else, we have had a great time poring over the pictures and recalling and reminiscing over various times and situations. As usual, these photos all look like people we knew, but it is somehow disorienting to look at them, but familiar, also. The brain is an amazing organ. Pick up a photo, and immediately there are conversations recalled. You remember what you were doing, why the photo was important to take at the time. The photos from Viet Nam, of course, provoke all kinds of thoughts. Did this guy make it? Did that guy ever get straightened out? Whatever happened to so-and-so? What-the-hell were we thinking here? How did we wind up there, and how on Earth are we still normal?

As we sat and looked over all this evidence of our post-adolescent lives, I thought of all the places, things, friends, occurrences that DJ and I have shared and experienced together. We only talk about those from a 'remember when' basis. Both of us are too macho to get too far in to…shit…I just don't have the talent to explain this. If we (you and I) were talking in real life, I could just start and then trail off a bit and you would help me finish the thought. Sitting here, I can 'see' what I want to say, and even envision what I mean, but there is just no way to put it in text. At least, not without pulling down or stepping in front of a lot of walls that have been erected over the years. DJ probably has the same thoughts regarding all this crap, but, as dudes, we just can't put a voice to them, I suppose.

There are so many stories in these pictures, and a lot more that are not directly represented here. You just don't carry cameras everywhere, and some situations just don't prompt you to reach for one, anyway. This is getting too introspective. I have tried to maintain a journal of some sort over the years, but I am remiss in consistent recording. Seems like I just don't have the sort of quiet times that are conducive to sitting down and writing all the time."

During the time we spoke, Ron was one of forty volunteers, mostly FBI agents, past and present, who followed former Green Beret colonel James "Bo" Gritz into the North Carolina woods on a weeklong mission to try to locate Eric Robert Rudolph, the Atlanta bomber. This was on August 15, 1998. Gritz was a right-wing militia leader who had persuaded survivalist Randy Weaver to abandon Ruby Ridge after a showdown with federal authorities in 1992.

When we first began chatting, Ron was not married, but was romantically involved with "the lovely Julie Dooley," a widow who lived next door to him in Washington. Her first husband had dropped dead of a heart attack on the driveway of their house next door. Julie and Ron had become romantically involved over the ensuing months. Julie was a special education teacher and she and Ron eventually decided to marry.

Ron had been married once before, to a girl from out East. They had a daughter together. When his wife left with their infant daughter, he signed off on letting his daughter be adopted by her new step-father. He claimed to have come home from an undercover mission and found a note on the kitchen counter explaining that his wife and child were gone for good. Why he did not follow them he never said. He talked about his lifestyle not being conducive to marriage, but, other than that, I never knew the real explanation.

His daughter was now grown and married, with a child of her own. DJ set about finding her (with Julie's full knowledge and cooperation) and "surprising" Ron by flying her to Dad's second wedding. In my world, these kinds of things don't happen. But they could and did in the world of DJ and Ron.

Eventually, over the years (five or so) that we spoke online, Ron retired under pressure from the DEA, married Julie, and, soon afterwards, right after the roadblock episode gone awry, his illness was discovered during the routine physicals that were caused by the broken leg. He refused medical treatment for the tumor for a long time, fearing that any surgery would leave him impaired. But, as DJ put it, "he heard Gabriel's trumpet blowing too loudly" and, after much delay and much investigation, Ron underwent experimental laser surgery on the tumor.

The surgery seemed to have been successful, at first. I still remember the one-line e-mail he sent post-surgery: "I'm back in the saddle again!" Certainly it beat taping a jeweler's loupe to his bad eye, so that he could see the screen in CarChat!

Ron died of a massive stroke soon after the apparently successful surgery. His wife found him on the floor, next to the computer, which was still on. DJ scattered Ron's ashes over Lake Wenatchee and helped his new bride—- now widowed for the second time—-with the disposition of Ron's cars and other accumulated properties. Ron had been setting things in order and being very fatalistic for the last year or so of his life. The end, while sudden, did not come as a total shock. I had been quoting the Dylan Thomas poem "Rage! Rage against the dying of the light!" to him, to no avail. I always wondered if, had he begun treatment sooner, the prognosis might have been different.

I also always wondered if Ron ever had a chance to transcribe his journal, or if Julie would do it for him post-mortem, as a final act of love.

During our online friendship, Ron sent me a poem or two, with the notation that they were "not yet finished." He always planned to write his *own* book. I wish he were alive to do just that.

Since he is not, I want to record for posterity two poems. The first, he claimed, was "not finished:"

You accuse me of having a heart that is bare,
And state that my capacity for feeling is spare,
But, until you have moved through the tunnels I've walked,
And spake with the souls with whom I have walked,
And until you have hung o'er the chasm of death
With nary a hope 'cept for just one more breath.

You cannot imagine the feeling of fear
As the principal tells you a policeman is here
Something has happened out on the road
And your life has just emptied of all that you hold.
And until you have stood in stony resolve
And you know that your world will never revolve,
In quite the way that it did up till now
And you don't understand the why and the how.

And if you've never held the head of a friend,
Embraced in your arms as he bleeds to his end,

103

Connie Corcoran Wilson

And committed his corpse to a hasty-dug hole,
Then prayed to his God to welcome that soul…
That never expected to die in some battle,
With the fear of his fate in his final sigh's rattle…

And if you haven't placed your life in the hands
Of another like you who is barely a man,
As you careen through the air on your mission of death,
Wondering which will be your last breath
As the lances of fire from the faceless below
Explode 'round your craft like the devil's light show…"

This was written on 12/19/96. He ended it with, "More later; this is not enough." There was not to be much more for Ron Whitley. He had little time left when he wrote it.

The other poem is entitled **"The Man in the Doorway."** I do not say that it is Ron's. Its author is unknown.

They came in low and hot,
Close to the trees
And dropped their tail in a flare,
Rocked forward
And we raced for the open doorways.
This was always the worst for us;
We couldn't hear anything
And our backs were turned to the tree line.
The best you could hope for was a sign
On the face of the man in the doorway,
Leaning out.
Waiting to help with a tug,
Or to lay down some lead.

Sometimes you could glance quickly at his face
And pick up a clue as to what was about to happen
We would pitch ourselves in headfirst and tumble
Against the scuffed riveted aluminum,
Grab for a handhold.
And will the son-of-a-bitch into the air.

Sometimes the deck was slick with blood—-or worse,
Sometimes something had been left in the shadows
Under the web seats, and sometimes they landed
In a shallow river to wash them out.
Sometimes they were late, sometimes…
They were parked in some other LZ
With their rotors turning a lazy arc,
A ghost crew strapped in once too often,
Motionless, waiting for their own lift,
Their own bags, once too often into the margins.
The getting on and the getting off were the worst for us
But this was all he knew,
The man in the doorway.

He was always standing in the noise,
Watching, urging…
Swinging out with his gun,
Grabbing the black plastic and heaving
Leaning out and spitting,
Spitting the taste away,
As though it would go away.

They came in low and hot,
Close to the trees
And dropped their tail in a flare,

Rocked forward
And began to kick the boxes out,
Bouncing against the skids, piling up on each other,
Food and water and bullets…
One thousand pounds of C's,
Warm water and rounds, 7.62 mm, half a ton of life and
death.
And when the deck was clear, we would pile the bags,
Swing them against their weight,
And throw them through the doorway,
His doorway, onto his deck.
And nod and he'd speak into that little mike,
And they'd go nose down
And lift into their last flight, their last extraction.

Sometimes, he'd raise a thumb,
Or perhaps a fist, or sometimes
Just a sly, knowing smile
Knowing we were staying and he was going.
But also knowing he'd be back,
He'd be back in a blink,
Standing in the swirling noise and the rotor wash,
Back to let us rush through his door
And skid across his deck
And will the son-of-a-bitch into the air.

They came in low and hot
Close to the trees,
And dropped their tail in a flare,
Rocked forward,
Kicked out the boxes
And slipped the litter across the deck.

And sometimes he'd lean down and hold the IV
And brush the dirt from a bloodless face,
Or hold back the flailing arms and the tears,
A thumbs-up to the right seat.
And you're only minutes away
From the white sheets,
The saws,
And the plasma.

They came in low and hot,
Close to the trees,
And dropped their tail in a flare,
Rocked forward.
And we'd never hear that sound again without feeling
Our stomachs go just a bit weightless,
Listen just a bit closer for the gunfire
And look up for the man in the doorway.

R.I.P., Rat.

Gold Above Dross

His work, he said, made relationships hard,
Fleeting glimpses in the night,
Many meetings in the day,
With travel and the rest of it,
He never got the chance to say
Anything that really mattered,
Anything that smacked of "deep."
All he did was flirt and natter,
Bed them well; then go to sleep.
He knew, in some remaining pocket,
Of what, at one time, was his soul,
That this was not what he was seeking,
Not the thing to make him whole.

She saw, because her sight was special,
That she could change the dice for him——
Transcend time and past and distance,
Take the words and make them sing.
She could put her soul on paper:
Thoughts and hopes, dreams and feelings.
Risking all: courageous thing!
All it took was love and bravery,
Time and hope and tender heart.
It would be a risky venture,
"But," she thought, "it is a start."

So, she did it, in her spare time
And other times that weren't so "spare,"
Wrapped it in a veil of kindness,

Offered it, the lady fair,
There it was: a gift worth giving,
Labor of love, investment of time,
Offering things he said he looked for:
Body, heart, soul and spirit,
Passion, wit, and first-rate mind.

He took the gift and turned it over,
Shook it once and kicked it twice,
Read the words that told it purely,
Skimmed the story, caressed the dice.
All the while that he was reading,
Continuing to shake the dice.

"Roll them!" he heard her say—-
But dimly,
Like a man within a trance.
She hoped he would waken—-
Roll them quickly; seize the moment; join the dance.
He almost did, but, for he knew it,
He'd forgotten how to be,
Remembering only "flirt and natter,"
No faith; no truth; no honesty.

She softly touched the gift she'd sent him,
Tattered, battered, tossed aside,
Looked at the words, from deep within her,
Sad and hurt, with smarting pride.
Part of her sobbed at the thought of betrayal,
That "boring" was all he could finally say.
But part of her knew that the fault was not hers,
Some piece of him long lost in the fray,

109

Some sort of obstacle blocking the way.

What part of him was gone, was wanting?
What quality did his heart lack?
Was it hope or trust or honor?
Could he ever get it back?
She knew that these she had and then some—-
These she had, with much to spare,
But he had none; he was not tender—-
Had no way to trust or share.
These she wished him for the future,
When he would realize his loss,
This she hoped he'd find forever
Choosing gold above the dross.

The Bar Czar

A friend of ours who fancies himself an entrepreneur we have dubbed "the Bar Czar," in honor of one of his more normal schemes, joint ownership of a bar. That project was fairly ordinary by the Bar Czar's standards.

Some of his schemes, like his fleet of chimney sweeps, his home-designed and produced sailboat, or his Bunkie Hunt phase, during which he invested heavily in silver, were amusing to me. The sailboat idea (he had never sailed, nor did he know anyone who sailed) gave way to a project involving the making and selling of religious icons. Then he had one involving doing local publicity for others by mailing things from home.

There was also the photoelectric cell, which was designed to trigger lights from outside a building, for use whenever police drove by to check a vacant supermarket or liquor store. This, he figured, was a fool-proof crime deterrent, as the lights would come on as the cops cruised by. It never saw the light of day—-no pun intended.

I thought of the entrepreneurial tendencies of my own family. Dad once had the opportunity to buy Winnebago stock at the very beginning of the company. He chose, instead, to invest in a Canadian mutual fund which had the distinction of being the only mutual fund that year to founder on the rocks of capitalism.

Mother decreed, in her infinite wisdom, that TV was "just a fad." Her exact words, "Pictures were never meant to fly through the air." She invested, instead, in a copper mine in Bolivia that was soon confiscated by the government. Mother's feeling that TV was a passing fad explains why I had to watch "Captain Video and His Video-Rangers" at Leah Hunter's house, all those years ago in my youth, when Tobor, the Robot, was doing his thing. We didn't have a television set until I was in high school, long after everyone else had one.

Mother always claimed to have predicted Pearl Harbor days in advance, and, therefore, thought that *all* her predictions were right on target.

Continuing the family tradition of dabbling in economic disaster, I was advised by my broker to buy tax-free municipal bonds, when what I, a movie buff, *really* wanted to do was to invest in a movie production firm called Delphi I.

After I followed the "safe" course of action outlined by my broker, and invested in the bonds, Delphi I—that fly-by-night investment opportunity that my broker advised me against—-made money hand over fist with 38 % ownership of the blockbuster movie "Tootsie!"

I also must own up to buying LTV Steel stock just before that company went totally bankrupt, taking 6,000 employees in Ohio, Indiana and Illinois down with it. Worse yet, my son was one of those employees.

I used to make fun of the Bar Czar's schemes, with chimney sweeps, sailboats and religious icons, but the other day he confided that he had never lost money on an investment. With my family's track record in money matters, maybe he knows something that I don't know!

From the "Truth is Stranger Than Fiction" File

Recently, a local radio station (KBOB) offered anyone who would agree to have the station's call letters tattooed on their forehead $150,000 apiece. Or so say David Winkleman of Davenport and his twenty-one-year-old step-son, Richard Goddard, Jr. The two men talked to station representatives and then proceeded to have KBOB tattooed across their foreheads. This made them in to walking billboards.

After that, things went horribly awry. The station reneged on the alleged monetary award, claiming that was not the offer. Mr. Goddard lost his job and said that he could not find other employment because he had KBOB tattooed on his forehead. A civil lawsuit was filed by Mr. Goddard against the radio station, but he failed to appear for a January 31, 2003, deposition or another motion hearing on February 13, 2003. So, things in court are pretty much going nowhere.

Somehow, Mr. Goddard ended up living in the Kershaw Trailer Park in Colona, Illinois, with John and Mary Rushman, ages 47 and 44. I guess they were friends of his. He complained so much about his bad luck that his hosts decided to "teach him a lesson" by stringing him up over a ceiling beam in their trailer. With friends like these, who needs enemies?

Now, here is where things get sticky. I once read a Janet (Harridan) Daily romance novel where they hung a horse. At the point in the plot where they were stringing up the horse, I had to stop and think about the logistics of hanging a horse in a barn. I could never figure out how that was possible. I did not recover sufficiently to read the rest of the book, I must admit.

Along those same lines, I am still thinking about most trailers I am aware of and wondering.....ceiling beams? My impression of most trailers is that they are not very tall structures. But, hey! I've never been to the Rushmans' trailer. And, with any luck, I never will have that experience. I still wonder how you can hang someone inside a trailer. Indeed, perhaps you cannot, because Mr. Goddard is still alive and kicking, although he did have to spend two nights in a local hospital.

The Rushmans, always the perfect hosts, also beat David Goddard Jr. with a ball-peen hammer while trying to hang him. Mrs. Goddard (Mary) is charged with aggravated battery for allegedly hitting Mr. Goddard in the right arm with the hammer while he was wrestling with her husband, John.

Mr. Rushman (John) is charged with aggravated battery for allegedly hitting Mr. Goddard in the face with the hammer, a second count of aggravated battery for attempting to hang David Goddard (Mr. Goddard subsequently spent two days in the hospital), a third count of aggravated battery for allegedly pushing a police officer and one count of criminal damage to state property for allegedly kicking the window out of a Colona police car. A misdemeanor count of resisting arrest was also filed against Mr. Rushman.

Both of the Rushmans have pleaded guilty to the charges and, as of this writing, are free on bond. They are scheduled to appear for a pre-trial hearing on July 17, 2003. If I were you, I would not complain around them.

What have we learned from this news story, boys and girls? Don't listen to radio stations that advertise big bucks if you will do something stupid, because the station might not pay off? Never try to hang something or someone in a structure that isn't tall enough? Don't drink while around someone with KBOB tattooed on his forehead? Don't complain if you *have* KBOB tattooed on your forehead?"

I'm not sure what the lesson to be learned here is. But I am sure there *is* one. Furthermore, I'll bet that it is a lesson that Sonny Morris and David Goddard, Jr., should really try to learn.

Left to right, on couch: Husband Craig Kenneth Wilson; daughter Stacey Kristin Corcoran Wilson; author Connie (Corcoran) Wilson; seated in front, son Scott Kevin Wilson and daughter-in-law Jessica (Henderson) Wilson. **Thanksgiving, 2003.**

The End

(Or, as the French are fond of saying, "À bientôt!")

You've now looked at life from *Both Sides Now*

Would you like to share this book with a friend? (**Sure, you would; you *know* you would!**) If so, you can order by phone, online, or by snail mail. Snail mail orders should fill out the information below, detach it, and mail it to:

1stBooks Library
1663 Liberty Drive, Suite #200
Bloomington, IN 47401

To order BY PHONE, call: 1-888-280-7715 or visit www.1stbooks.com **ONLINE**
OR
detach the form below, after figuring charges due, and enclose check, money order or credit card information (Visa, MasterCard) and mail to the address given above. (*Illinois residents: add 6.25% sales tax, or $1.25 per hardcover book and .98 per paperback book.)

Hardcover books, per copy, are $20.00. Paperback books, per copy, are $15.75.
Shipping costs, per book(s) ordered, via UPS are as follows:

1 book = $5.75	6 books = $10.50
2 books = $6.75	7 books = $10.75
3 books = $7.50	8 books = $11.00
4 books = $8.00	9 books = $11.25
5 books = $8.50	10 books = $11.50

DETACH HERE: (Fill this out if you wish to charge, and then continue to fill out the information regarding number of books, postage, tax).
Credit card I wish to use (circle one) VISA   Mastercard

Name on credit card: _____

Credit card number: _____

Expiration date: _____

Total Amount charged: _____

_____

For those enclosing check or money order fill in the information below and enclosed with your check or money order; credit card orders must fill out BOTH sections:

Number of books ordered: _____ @ _____ (please circle whether paperback or hardcover). Cost per book (see above): _____

Postage/handling: _____

Illinois sales tax (if applicable): _____ Total Amount Enclosed: _____

Sample Order(s):

Sample Order Number One:

Number of books ordered: ___5 @ $20.00_____ (please circle whether paperback or hardcover)
Cost per book: __$20.00_____

Postage/Handling: ____$8.50_____

Illinois sales tax ($1.25 per book):____$6.25_____

Total Amount Enclosed:__$114.75_____

Sample Order Number Two (non-Illinois resident):

Number of books ordered:__3_____ @ ___$15.75_____ (please circle whether paperback or hardcover)

Cost per book:_$15.75

Postage/handling:_$7.50

Illinois sales tax (.98 per book): ___N.A._____

Total Amount Enclosed:_$54.75

(*Note: Please remember that, if ordering by credit card, BOTH sections must be filled out and mailed in. Thank you.)